GREENBERG'S®
AMERICAN FLYER S GAUGE
1945 - 1965
REPAIR AND OPERATING MANUAL

SECOND EDITION

THOMAS B. BARKER

Greenberg Publishing Company, Inc.
Sykesville, Maryland

Copyright © 1983
Thomas B. Barker

Greenberg Publishing Company, Inc.
7566 Main Street
Sykesville, Maryland 21784
(410) 795-7447

First Edition
Third Printing

Manufactured in the United States of America

Greenberg Publishing Company, Inc., publishes the world's largest selection of Lionel, American Flyer, LGB, Marx, Ives, and other toy train publications as well as a selection of books on model and prototype railroading, dollhouse building, and collectible toys. For a complete listing of current Greenberg publications, please call 1-800-533-6644 or write to Kalmbach Publishing Co., 21027 Crossroads Circle, Waukesha, Wisconsin 53187.

Greenberg Shows, Inc., sponsors *Greenberg's Great Train, Dollhouse and Toy Shows*, the world's largest of their kind. The shows feature extravagant operating train layouts and a display of magnificent dollhouses. The shows also present a huge marketplace of model and toy trains, for HO, N, and Z Scales; Lionel O and Standard Gauges; S, and 1 Gauges; plus layout accessories and railroadiana. They also offer a large selection of dollhouse miniatures and building materials, and collectible toys. Shows are scheduled along the East Coast each year from Massachusetts to Florida. For a list of our current shows, please call (410) 795-7447 or write to Greenberg Shows, Inc., 7566 Main Street, Sykesville, Maryland 21784 and request a show brochure.

Greenberg Auctions, a division of Greenberg Shows, Inc., offers nationally advertised auctions of toy trains and toys. Please contact our auction manager at (410) 795-7447 for further information.

ISBN 89778-017-5

Library of Congress Cataloging-in-Publication Data

Barker, Thomas B.
    Greenberg's American Flyer S Gauge Operating & Repair Manual.
        1. Railroads — Models. I. Greenberg, Linda. II. Title III. Title:
American Flyer S Gauge Operating & Repair Manual.
TF197.B24 1983   625.1'9   83-16342
ISBN 0-89778-017-5

TABLE OF CONTENTS

Cover Photograph by Roger Bartelt
Text Photographs by Tom Barker
Line Diagrams by Trip Riley

AT THE THROTTLE

Tom Barker's apprenticeship in American Flyer repair work began when he was eleven. He had received a 342 for Christmas which was broken — it had been purchased at half price of course because of its condition — and he set out to make it run. And run it did.

Around 1972 Tom's interest in AF revived when he discovered that A. C. Gilbert had gone out of business. He then began to acquire engines, rolling stock and accessories and by 1973 found himself building an extensive layout for his equipment. He also began to write a "Roundhouse" column for the **S Gaugian** magazine and then became involved in other AF writing projects (a price guide and repair manual).

When not in the Roundhouse Tom works as a Project Leader with Xerox's Reprographic Technology Department and teaches Statistics at the Rochester Institute of Technology (RIT). He has a Bachelors in Photographic Science and a Masters in Statistics from RIT.

Tom, his wife Anne, his daughter Audrey and son Greg live in Webster, New York. His mailing address is: 1223 Lake Point Drive, Webster, N.Y. 14580

PREFACE

To my children, Audrey and Greg, and to all children who will inherit and preserve the train legacy left by A.C. Gilbert.

When the A. C. Gilbert Co. went out of business in early 1967, those of us who had grown up with American Flyer (AF) trains felt as if we had lost a dear friend. Although the company changed hands in the early 1960s, the network of authorized service stations had continued to keep our trains speeding down the main line.

Now it's up to us to preserve the heritage created by A. C. Gilbert and keep the trains running on our layouts or around the annual Christmas tree.

Unfortunately, many people are afraid to try their hand at repair work and they sometimes think that they will end up with a pile of parts that just won't go back together. Then there are those who are quite expert in train repair, but still run into a problem that has a prized engine on the bench for days. In any case, an efficient plan of attack in an orderly fashion can help the beginner as well as the expert get to the heart of the problem with the least disassembly and frustration.

I believe . . . and experience has shown . . . that anyone, with a little guidance, can take an engine apart, diagnose, locate and correct the problem. I repaired my first engine when I was only 11! Operating AF trains is a wonderful and relaxing pleasure that draws us all to the hobby. When our trains are in good repair, their promise of fun is fulfilled. I hope that this Guide is as useful to you as it is to me in restoring AF trains and accessories to their former glory.

To help the neophyte gain familiarity with terms and methods, the first two chapters present tools and parts. The chapters on operation are distilled from the Gilbert Instruction Sheets or instruction books. In all cases, I have tried to clearly explain why a procedure should be followed rather than just tell you what to do. I firmly believe that this will help you solve your immediate problem and provide understanding for future unique train problems should they arise.

Thomas B. Barker

Since the first edition of Tom Barker's Repair and Operating Manual went out-of-print, we have had constant inquiries as to when the book would be available again. We are very pleased that this interest has not waned and, in fact, it would appear that the commitment to American Flyer has never been stronger. This edition of the Manual is essentially the same as the first with some important additions. The original American Flyer schematics WITH their parts lists are included as are more how-to repair or how-to diagnose operating problems, particularly in the accessories chapter.

Again, we proudly note that Tom Barker's dedication to the care and preservation of American Flyer equipment and his willingness to share his insights and knowledge have made this book possible.

Linda Greenberg
August 20, 1983

Chapter I

TOOLS AND PARTS

American Flyer (AF) locomotives and accessories were mass produced and are simple machines designed to be easily assembled.* You will probably find, when planning train repair work, that you already have the basic tools of the trade. However, it is important to have all the necessary tools within reach when you begin to disassemble these fine machines.

Table 1 lists the essential tools that you should have. Those that have an asterisk (*) in front of them are helpful, but not necessary, and could be added at a later date.

Table I-1

Essential Tools and Supplies

*AC Ammeter, 0-5 amps
 Cleaning Solvent (not gasoline)
 Clip Leads, pair
 Cottom Swabs (Q-tips)
 Cyanoacrylate Glue, such as Eastman 910
 Diagonal Cutters
 Engine Holder (you will need to build it)
 Epoxy Cement
 Epoxy Putty
 Fine File or Sandpaper Stick
 Light Grease, such as Lubriplate
 Light Oil, "3 in 1"
 Long Nose Pliers
*Nut Drivers, with 3/16 and 1/4-inch drivers
 Sandpaper, #400 or #600
 Screwdrivers, with 1/8, 3/16 and 5/16-inch blades
 Screws, assorted lengths of #4-40 and #6-32
*Silicone Spray
 Solder, 60/40
 Soldering Pencil, 25-40 watts
 Toothbrushes, the old, soft, worn-out variety
 TV Tuner Cleaner
 Tweezers, 4 inches long
*Volt Ohm Meter (VOM), such as Radio Shack's #22-204
 Wheel Puller (you will need to make one)
*Wire Stripper, for 18, 20 and 22 gauge wires

Before using these tools, we will examine them to make sure that you apply each as intended for the job at hand.

Although a **screwdriver** may seem a fairly straightforward and simple tool, its improper use could damage an engine's original screws. Obviously, a big screwdriver will not fit into a small screw, but a small blade which loosely fits into a large screw can damage the screw slot. Be sure to select the screw driver that most comfortably fits into the screw slot.

A **magnetic screwdriver** can help when you have to get a screw into a tight place, such as the underside of a tender. You can buy a magnetic screwdriver, or make one by simply taking an ordinary screwdriver and magnetizing it. To

magnetize a screwdriver wind about 100 turns of #20 or #22 insulated wire around the shank of the screwdriver and attach the wire ends to the base post and to the 7-15 volt posts of your AF transformer. Using the speed control, turn the voltage on and off gradually, then check the screwdriver for magnetism. If the screwdriver will not pick up a screw, repeat the process again. Alternating current from your transformer may make the task more difficult, but you usually will succeed on the first or second try. The trick is to catch the polarity in mid-stream and thus hold the magnetism. For more reliable results use direct current instead of alternating current.

To demagnetize the screwdriver, strike the blade on a hard surface so as to physically randomize the magnetic poles.

One tool that is often oversold is the **soldering iron**. While there are some hefty 100-watt-plus soldering guns available, I am not sure what good purpose they can be used for. They do not have enough power for plumbing, and they produce too much heat for train repairs. The best size soldering iron is the 25-40 watt **soldering pencil**. It is also ideal for printed circuit board work if you are interested in electronic projects.

Although you can begin to repair trains without owning electrical meters, you will find that an **ammeter** connected in series with your test track makes a great diagnostic tool. Since such a meter is costly, you may wish to wait to purchase one. If you do decide to spend some money on a meter, I would suggest that you first buy a **Multi Meter** or **Volt Ohm Meter** (VOM). If you watch for a sale you should be able to pick one up for $25-$30 or less. The VOM should have a good 1X ohms scale so that you can read 30 ohms accurately. This is a great help in repairing smoke units. You can also construct a **makeshift ammeter** with your VOM. You will need a 1 ohm,10 watt resistor, available at any radio supply store.

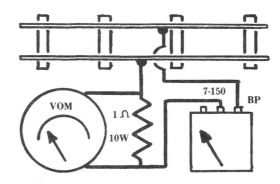

Figure I-1   Make-shift Ammeter

Connect the resistor in series with the test track and measure the voltage drop across the resistor with your VOM. Figure I-1 shows the wiring diagram. Since the current in a series circuit is constant and the voltage drop is measured across a 1 ohm resistor, you have 2.5 amps in the circuit if you read 2.5 volts across the resistor using your VOM. A word of caution, the reading will be correct as long as the resistor remains at 1 ohm. The heat generated by the current flowing through the resistor will cause the current to change because the resistance has changed. So, use the makeshift ammeter for only brief periods and only when the resistor is cool.

---

* A simple machine is, according to Webster, one of six or more mechanisms formerly considered elements composing all machines: 1) lever, (2) inclined plane, (3) wheel and axle, (4) screw, (5) pulley and (6) wedge.

Your choice of lubricants is vital to the smooth running and life of your equipment. Use a light oil such as a 3 in 1 or sewing machine oil and do not use too much. Excess oil does not cause motors to run more smoothly. Just the reverse, excess oil only inhibits the flow of electricity. Half a drop is quite sufficient.

When it comes to a **grease**, do not use the yellowish-brown material packed with the AF #26 Service Kit. It has a tendency to harden and slow down the drive train. Save it as a collector's item and use a modern lubricant such as **Lubriplate**.

Another modern material, an adhesive, now commonly found on hardware store shelves, does a superior job of sticking metals and plastics together. Developed a number of years ago by the Eastman Kodak Company, this glue carries the proper name of **Cyanoacrylate**, but can be purchased under the brand names of "Super Glue," "Alpha Iron" or "Eastman 910." The package warns of the dangers in using this adhesive; it will stick skin together as rapidly as it cements metal and plastic, so do not spill it on yourself. Acetone (nail polish remover) will dissolve the glue and a small bottle should be kept handy for an emergency. Be sure to read the label before using it. Cyanoacrylates have a shelf life of three months or less once opened. To prolong its life, keep the tube cool by storing in a refrigerator. When the glue is no longer useful, it is not runny and you may as well discard it, since its sticking properties are no longer there.

Besides the ammeter, there are two other tools that you can build to make your train repairs more professional. The first, a **padded locomotive holder**, is easily constructed from a few pieces of scrap lumber and some soft cloth. Figure I-2 shows a padded locomotive holder. The idea here is to build two walls lined with soft cloth to hold the engine while you remove the screws. The screws are then placed into the cups so that they do not inadvertently get lost or fall onto the floor. I built my holder with two 15 inch 2x4s attached to a 10x12 piece of 3/8-inch plywood. The cups to hold screws are artists' mixing cups purchased from an art store.

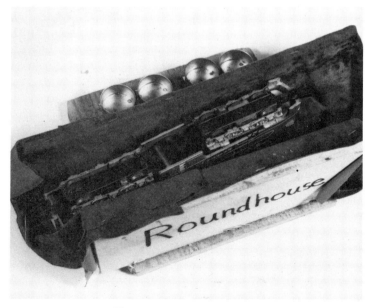

Figure I-2   Locomotive Holder

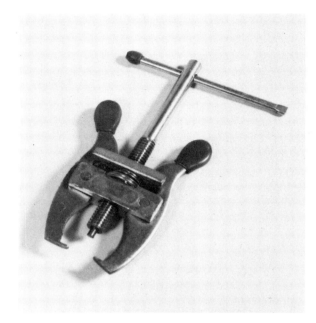

Figure I-3   Wheel Puller

If you need to remove the wheels from any engine, whether steamer or diesel, a **wheel puller** is useful to help you do the job without damaging the wheel. You can make a wheel puller by modifying a battery cable puller. A battery cable puller can be purchased in an automotive store or department for less than $3 and the modifications required are quite simple. First, remove the pad on the end of the puller by turning the screw back until it pops off. This will leave the threaded screw part of the puller free. Next, cut off one end of the T-bar handle and remove the handle. This will allow you to chuck the non-threaded end in a 3/8-inch electric drill. Start the drill which has been held down securely and grind the tip of the threaded rod to a 1/16-inch diameter, about 3/8-inch back. Use a fine, sharp file to grind the tip. You can test the diameter by checking to see if the tip will pass through the center hole in the engine wheel. Use an old wheel as a guide.

The next step in constructing your $3 wheel puller is to file or grind down (if you have a bench grinder) the hooked ends of the battery cable puller so they will fit between the back of the wheel and the engine chassis. Do not file the ends down too far or you will weaken them. About 3/64 of an inch should suffice. The last step is to screw the threaded part back into the puller and reinsert the handle. Flatten the end of the handle to keep it from sliding out. Figure I-3 shows the finished puller.

While tools for AF repairs can be easily obtained or made to order, original parts are becoming scarce. There is nothing more frustrating than diagnosing a problem and learning that only a new part will repair the piece. In some cases, it is possible to obtain new parts. Some are original factory replacements and some are remanufactured. Sometimes the only solution is for you to manufacture a part. Throughout this book, I will suggest ways of making repairs other than replacing a broken part with a new one. Salvage whatever is possible and sometimes whatever seems impossible is the only rational philosophy in a dwindling parts market.

Plastic parts seem particularly vulnerable and subject to breakage, but you can easily make replacement parts for them. Many a passenger car has been found for sale on a bargain table with broken steps or skirts. To restore a broken step or skirt you need only make a mold of the good part,

Figure I-4   Parts Made From Rubber Molds: Skirts, Milk
Cans, Observation Car Bezel, Mailbag, Cows, Hay
for Hay Ejector

Figure I-5 shows **field magnets** for AC motors. Figure I-6 shows the **commutator and armature assemblies** for the steam engines that evolved over the years in the Gilbert Plant. The **diesel armatures** are shown in Figure I-7.

Figure I-6   Steam Engine Armatures: Pre-PUll Mor, Standard
Pull Mor, Super Motor, Side Commutator and
Last Design from Inexpensive Engines

Figure I-7   Diesel Armatures: Early Straight Design, Slanted
Small and More Common Slanted Long Designs

attach it with cyanoacrylate glue and paint it to match. Presto! You now have a whole car for a fraction of the cost of the perfect specimen.

The mold can be made with a silicone rubber or bathtub caulk sold by GE or Dow-Corning. Remember to use a good **mold release wax**, such as "Insulator Wax" (made by the Collinite Chemical Co. of Utica, NY) or a high quality automobile wax, to coat the good part from which you are taking the impression. Next, spread a thin layer, about 1/32 of an inch, of the rubber and let it cure. Continue to spread thin layers until you have built the layers up to about one-quarter of an inch. Then pry the mold away from the original. Fill the mold with epoxy and let it set. The mold can be peeled away from the part since the silicone rubber does not stick to anything once it has cured. Treat your molds with care and you can reuse them many times.

I have used **silicone rubber molds** to make mail bags, cows, milk cans and baggage, and have used this method to repair broken steps or skirts on cars, engines and tenders. Making parts can be one of the most rewarding of repair and restoration activities. Figure I-4 shows an array of parts made from this rubber mold technique. The one-way cloth on the cows comes from the paint pad sold under the brand name of "Sure Line." The baggage square is simply a cube of solder.

I will next use a number of technical terms to describe the various parts of AF electric motors. For those who are not experts in the identification of these parts, the following pictures will help you locate some of the major motor parts.

The following dealers have parts lists available and can supply original and reproduction parts for AF trains. Those marked with an asterisk (*) have catalogues with parts pictured as well.

Table 1-2   Parts Suppliers

* Leventon's Hobby Supply P.O. Box 1525 Chehalis, WA 98532 (206) 748-3643	* Russ Burns 2109 Pineview Court Marilla, NY 14102 (716) 652-1110
* Triple "S" Supplies P.O. Box 343 Secane, PA 19018 (215) 436-8739	* Hobby Surplus Sales 287 Main Street P.O. Box 2170G New Britain, CT 06050 (203) 223-0600

To aid in the identification of engine parts and locations, reproductions of the Gilbert Factory Parts Lists for major steam and diesel engines are shown in the Parts List Appendix at the back of the Manual. These factory parts lists show the parts for every engine and most variations. Usually the parts are interchangeable and the basic, generic diagrams included here should allow you to identify needed parts and to order them from those suppliers that still have them for sale.

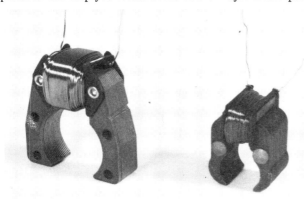

Figure I-5   AC Field Magnets: Steam (on the left) and Diesel
(on the right)

Chapter II

DIAGNOSING A PROBLEM

There is an old saying among automobile mechanics that goes something like this: "For every hour spent doing repair work, at least two hours were spent looking for and identifying the problem." I have often found this to be true of the more difficult AF repair problem, and therefore suggest that a systematic approach to discovering the problem is the best one to take.

This chapter provides diagnosing guidance. There is a **Trouble Shooting Flow Diagram** and specific diagnostic steps outlined to help you find a problem as quickly as possible. Remember that AF engines are simple machines and that only certain things can go wrong with them. By using an ammeter as your basic diagnostic tool and a little common sense you should be able to locate the problem and get your engine out of the roundhouse and back on the "high iron" in short order.

The following list, when coupled with the Trouble Shooting Flow Chart (Figure II-1), covers the common sources of engine problems.

Table II-1

Common Sources & Engine Problems

Problem	Enter Flow Diagram at Number
Causes direct short	1
Draws too much current (over three amps)	2
Drivers spark at turnouts	3
Goes only in reverse	1
No smoke	4
Refuses to run (no current)	1
Reverse unit is inoperative	1
Stop—go operation	1

To use the Trouble Shooting diagram, enter the Flow Diagram at the numbered point and answer the question in the diamond. If the answer indicates an action item, do it and then try the engine out. If the problem persists, go on to the next question and repeat the process until the engine is functioning properly.

In addition to using the Flow Chart, you should record what actions you take on the "Roundhouse Record" or data sheets (located at the back of this book). By keeping an engine log you will be able to save time on future repairs, since you will have a record of which items have been cleaned and/or which parts replaced or repaired for each engine.

Now that you understand the generalities of the trouble-shooting procedure, let us try out the process by taking a rather beat-up engine through the Flow Chart at point #1. We first inspect the pickup wheels and find a large accumulation of dirt compacted with thick oil on the metal tender pick up wheels. Our first job is to scrape off the accumulation with a small screwdriver. All the wheels are scraped clean, including the plastic ones, so that the dirt cannot be redeposited on the track, which would start the problem all over again after a short period of running. The metal wheels are then polished with very fine sandpaper or a wire brush.

When we place the engine back on the track, the reverse unit starts clicking, but the engine does not move. After removing the tender body we see that the reverse unit is also dirt-encrusted. A wiping with several Q-tips and an application of TV contact spray leaves us with a clean, sparkling and operative reverse unit.

Another test and the engine still does not run. This time we check the wires from the tender to the engine and find that one has broken off. We replace it with a flexible #26 or #28 wire of the proper length. This corrects the "no-run" condition, but we find we are drawing too much current, over three amps.

To get to the root of this problem, remove the boiler from the steam engine and examine the motor. The commutator is gunked-up with oil residue and brush filings. The oil should be wiped off with another Q-tip and the filings in the commutator air gaps removed with a toothpick. Check the length of the brushes. These are one-quarter of an inch, so they are long enough to make good contact.

On the worm gear we find a considerable amount of hard grease. It should be dissolved with a solvent and scraped away.

We observe that the wheels are solid so there are no tires that need our attention and we check out the smoke unit. It registers a reading of 40 ohms on our VOM. However, no smoke emerges when we run the engine, so we add some solvent in the filler hole to loosen the wick in the smoke unit. Finally, we reassemble the engine. It runs smoothly as great billows of smoke pour forth from the stack. Even though this engine had initially appeared a basket case, by approaching its problems logically, from the simplest to the more complex, we successfully performed the necessary steps with a minimum of disassembly. Keep that point in mind as you work on any engine, car or accessory. Do not take anything apart if you do not have to!

That was a preview of what we shall discuss in detail in the next chapters. At this point, I do not expect that you could do all of the above steps without first reading the chapters on engines, smoke units and reverse units. However, this chapter should serve as a guide as to how to apply the information you will gain in the rest of the book.

Figures II-2 through II-5 give more specific details for different engine types. You should refer to the general Flow Chart and to each of the diagnosis guides before tackling a problem engine.

In the diagnosis guides, problems are grouped as to whether they are mechanical or electrical. Again, the common problems are described and the most likely causes listed. This format should help you get to the root of the problem and to arrive at a solution more readily. Remember, use the Flow Chart to diagnose your engine's problem.

Figure II - 1

Trouble Shooting Flow Diagram

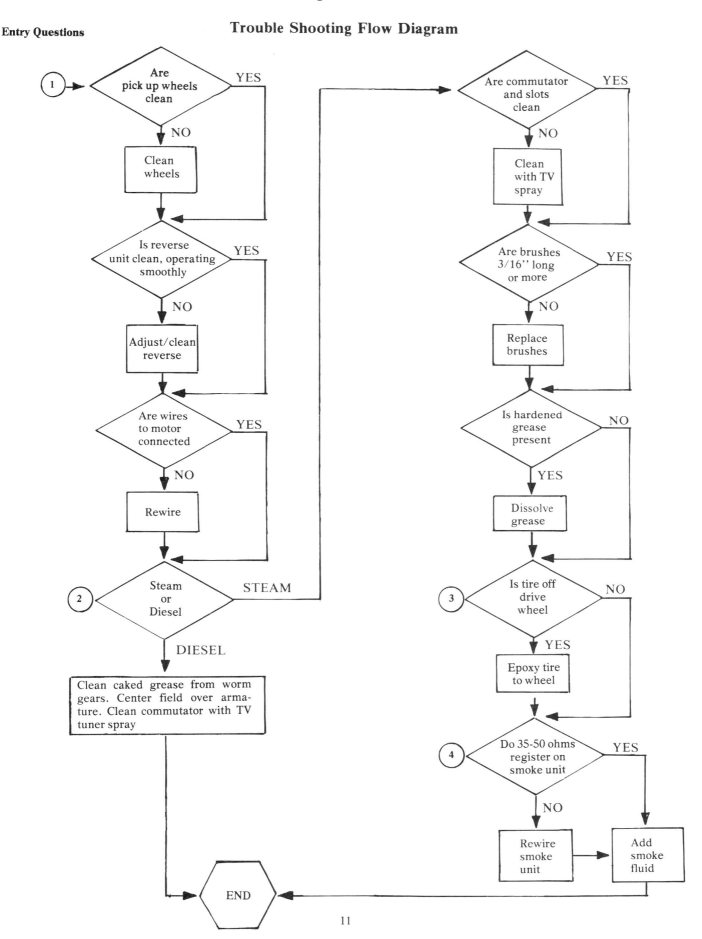

Figure II-3

Diagnosis Guide for Steam Engines

Problems:	Causes/Solutions	Tools
Electrical		
Current over 2.5 amps.	Wired incorrectly (usually will run in one direction only); armature or field shorted	Ammeter
No Current	Broken wires from tender; dirty pickup wheels; faulty reverse unit	Ammeter
Blows breaker	Wired incorrectly; wheels on backwards; "hot chassis" shorting through draw-bar	Transformer
	Open armature or field windings; brushes not contacting the commutator	
No Smoke	Nichrome wire burned out	None
Mechanical		
Runs only in reverse (forward erratic)	Armature thrust set incorrectly; brush springs not at one inch; worn rear armature bearing; wrong armature	None
Noisy	Too much brush tension; lack of lubrication, misaligned rear armature cap	None
Shorts on curve or switch	Drive wheels separated from tires	None
No choo-choo	Cylinder clogged	None
No smoke	Wick clogged. Use solvent to unclog	None

Tips

When operating Challenger 4-8-4 engines, make sure that the curved sections in your pike are not too sharp. If too sharp, add an extra one-half straight section to smooth it out so that your engine will not jump the track. Be sure pickup wheels on two-step reverse unit engines are clean to avoid unwanted reversing.

Figure II-4

Diagnosis Guide for Alco PA-1 and GP-7

Problems:	Causes/Solutions	Tools
Electrical		
Motors run, but engine does not move	Dual motors wired in opposition. Reverse field wires on one motor	None
No current	Dirty pickup wheels. Faulty fingers in reverse unit, broken wires, brush springs disconnected or weak, brushes jammed in holder	Ammeter
Excessive current (over 4 amps)	Wired incorrectly (runs in one direction only), rewound armature or field not insulated from chassis	Ammeter
No horn sound	Speaker burned out, capacitor open, horn control connected incorrectly	None
Mechanical		
Runs slowly High current	Elliptical hole worn into drive wheel bushings (the bushings should be circular with very little play)	Ammeter
Runs well in one direction and slowly or not at all in other direction	Field not centered	None
Motor starts only with push	Armature winding shorted or open	None
Plastic shell melts	Resistor for horn overheating (see below)	None

Tips

Remove resistor in horn unit to reduce crackling noises and to prevent the melting of the body shell. Use a 25mfd capacitor **only** for horn connection. For greater power with less overheating rewind fields with #26 rather than #28 wire. Use longer screws in worn screw holes.

Figure II-5	Figure II-6
Diagnosis Guide for Franklin & Washington Engines	**Diagnosis Guide for Baldwin Diesels**

Problems:	Causes/Solutions	Tools
Electrical		
Stops or reverses while running	Dirty pickup wheels on tender	None
Blows breaker	Wired incorrectly, wheels on backwards	Transformer
Current over 2.5 amps.	Shorted armature or field, or poor insulation	Ammeter
No Smoke	Smoke unit burned out, install new unit	None
Mechanical		
No Smoke	Wick clogged. Use solvent to unclog	None
Reverses while running	Tender too light (see tip below)	None
Noisy	Design characteristic, excessive noise can be reduced by proper lubrication	None
No choo-choo	Design characteristic	None

Tips

To keep the tender on the track, weight it down by adding fishing sinkers or other heavy material. This will keep the pickup wheels in contact with the track and prevent the two-step reverse unit from changing direction at the wrong time.

Problems:	Causes/Solutions	Tools
Electrical		
No current	Broken connection wires, dirty pickup wheels, faulty reverse unit, brushes not making contact with commutator	Ammeter
High current (over 3 amps)	Wired incorrectly (will run only in one direction), poor insulation on non-powered truck, shorted field or armature	Ammeter
Erratic current	Fiber washer missing from commutator end of armature	Ammeter
Mechanical		
High current, does not run, blows breaker	Armature touches field, brush and bearing cap bushing worn or plastic worn near bushing	Ammeter
Noisy	Drive wheel bushings worn	None

Tips

Rewind the field with heavier #26 enameled wire to reduce overheating and improve performance. Keep chassis bushings lubricated.

Chapter III

POWER TO THE ENGINE

Nearly three-quarters of the problems that bring an engine into the roundhouse are caused by faulty transmission of the electrical power to the worm drive motor. In this chapter, we detail the procedures for cleaning wheels, adjusting reverse units and rewiring.

Since steam engines are so numerous, we first describe the problems of getting power from the tender pickup wheels to the motor. Of course, many of these diagnostic ideas can be applied to diesels or to the only steam engine without a tender, the docksider.

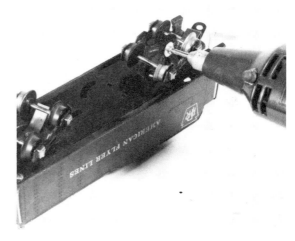

Figure III-2   Polishing Wheels

Figure III-1   Spreading Trucks Sides To Remove Wheels

DIRTY WHEELS

If the engine moves in jerks, stops, or reverses and then goes forward with a mind of its own, it is probably a case of dirty wheels. Remove the wheels from the tender by spreading the truck sides as shown in Figure III-1. Do not spread the sides too far out or you will break off the sintered side.

Clean the wheels with solvent. If the metal wheels have become pitted from arcing, a fine file should be used to smooth the surface. If you have an electric drill with a wire brush attachment, you can also polish the metal wheels. Do not try to polish the plastic wheels or the brush's abrasive action will chew them up. You can leave the metal wheels in the truck sides. A small motor tool, like a Dremel, with a wire brush-polisher also works very well, as shown in Figure III-2.

If you remove the wheels to clean them, be sure they are replaced properly. With the tender upside down and the front facing away from you, the metal wheels should be on the left side of the front truck and the right side of the rear truck. On each truck, the metal wheels should be on the same side. Do not have metal wheels crossed on the same truck. If you cross

the metal wheels there will be a direct short which will stop the train. Figure III-3 shows the proper wheel arrangement and also how the trucks' spring metal contacts go under the axles and make good electrical contact with the axles. Any accumulation of dirt and excess oil should be removed. A small amount of oil is helpful here as well as on the ends of the axles in the journal boxes. A **pinpoint oiler** is a good tool to use for this purpose. Wipe off any excess oil with a Q-tip.

Figure III-3   Proper Pick Up Wheel Arrangement

NOT CORRECT FOR A.F. STEAM ENGINE

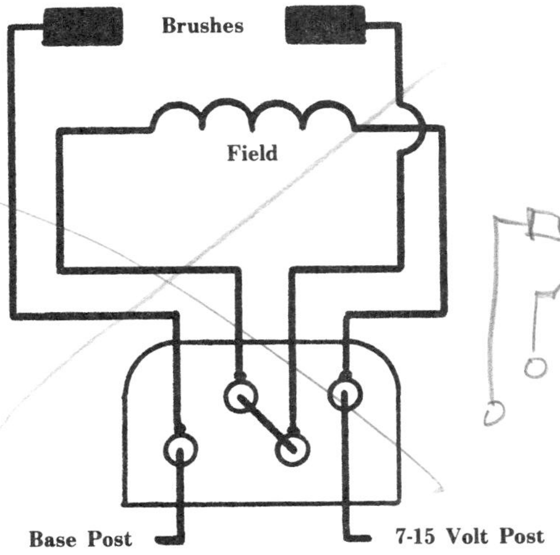

Brushes

Field

Base Post

7-15 Volt Post

Figure III-4   How to Make A Direct Connection To The
Motor Through The Jack Panel

REVERSE UNITS

Most of the four-step reverse units that came with the majority of AF steam engines are located in the tender. There is an alternate location in the engine itself for engines made before 1948. Pre and post 1948 units are alike and should be serviced in the same way—the only difference is in the disassembly technique. In the case of tender-mounted units you should first detach the tender from the engine, then detach the drawbar screw directly underneath the cab of the engine and unplug the wires from the engine. If there is a wire without a plug just above the plugged wires, unsolder it. In some later engines, the wires do not have a plug and working on the engine is a bit more difficult since you will not be able to detach the tender from the engine.

In most cases the tender can be detached and is easy to work on. Turn the tender over and remove the screws that secure the body to the chassis. The reverse unit is mounted on the chassis. A few tinplate tenders are held together with twisted metal clips. The clips can break off after a few twists, so it would be wise to decide **if** the unit really needs servicing before removing the tender body from the chassis. You can check it by testing the engine with a direct connection to the jack panel as shown in Figure III-4. If the engine runs with the direct connection, but not with the tender, you can be sure that either the reverse unit or the wiring is defective. If the engine does not run with the direct wire, there is still a chance that the wiring is defective or that the reverse unit is faulty. Considering the fragile tender connectors, it would be best to first fix the motor before taking the risk of snapping off the tender clips.

After opening the tender, clean the reverse unit with TV contact cleaner. Spray the fluid all over the unit to clean and lubricate the contacts and bearings. As you spray, rotate the drum by moving the reverse unit lock back and forth. Check to see if the cleaning has restored the reverse unit to proper operation. Put the tender on the track and connect the plug to the engine. If you hold the engine above the tracks, you need not worry that the engine will pull the wires away from the tender.

Flipping the solenoid bar up + down!

The next problem in getting power to the motor involves the wires connecting the reverse unit with the engine. If these wires are broken off at the plug, carefully strip off the insulation and find the fine wire. If only one wire is broken, it is easy to reconnect the correct wire to the plug. If more than one is missing, you will have to trace the wires from the reverse unit to the motor. The general wiring diagrams in Figure III-5 show the proper connections. To trace the wires, you will need either a VOM or a continuity tester as shown in Figure III-6. If you use the Volt Ohm Meter (VOM) set it on the X1 ohms position and, with the engine disconnected from the tender, place the reverse unit in the neutral position. In this position, the fingers of the reverse unit will rest on the plastic drum surface. Place one probe on the reverse unit end of the wire and check each of the wires on the other end until you find the correct one which will register zero on the meter. If you use a continuity tester, the bulb will light when you have found the wire.

When you resolder the wires back on the plug, first tin the strands by heating the wire and melting the solder onto them. Then hold your soldering iron on the metal part of the plug until the solder in the plug melts. Slip the tinned wire into the plug and remove the heat. Wait until the solder cools before letting go of the wire. You can avoid burning your fingers if you use a tweezers to hold the wire in place.

Once you have checked for wire continuity or rewired the reverse unit, you should check for the proper flow of current through the reverse unit fingers and drum. Figure III-7 shows how the reverse unit works to make the motor go forward. Figure III-8 shows the connections for reverse operation. You can see that the current must flow through the fingers and across the drum connection to get the engine moving. You can check the forward current in your engine by using your VOM or continuity tester. With the drum rotated so that the top two fingers on the reverse unit are connected, as shown in Figure III-9 you should get an indication of continuity. If you show no conduction, you have worn or bent fingers. If the fingers are badly worn, they will normally have to be replaced. Figure III-10 shows badly worn, repaired and new fingers. However,

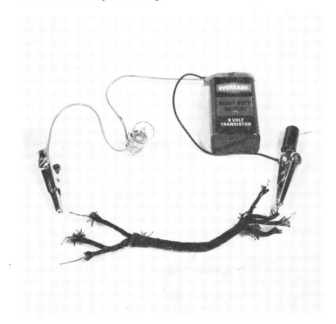

Figure III-6   **Continuity Tester**
Use a 14 volt lamp (#1449), two alligator clips and a 9 volt battery. When the lamp lights you have found the two ends of the wire.

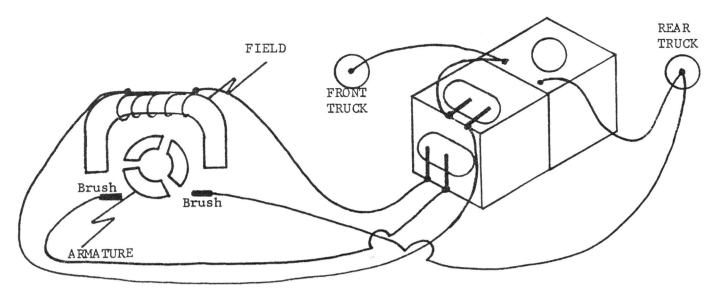

Figure III-5a   Wiring Diagram for Four-Step Reverse Unit

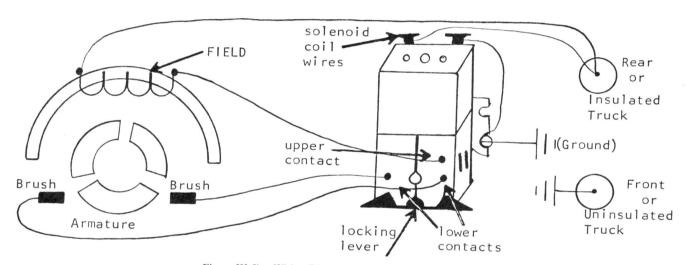

Figure III-5b   Wiring Diagram for Two-Step Reverse Unit

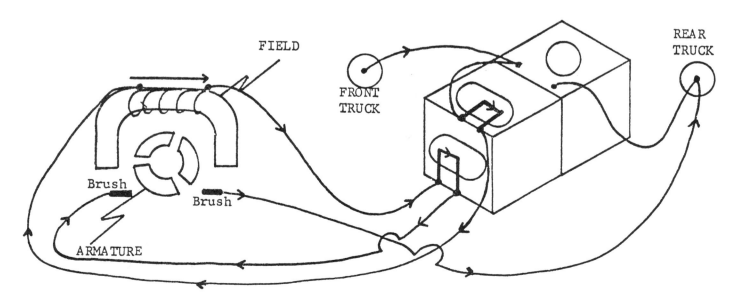

Figure III-7   Forward Wiring and Current Flow

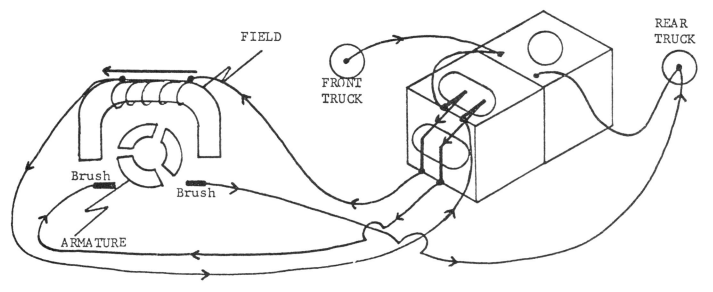

Figure III-8   Reverse Wiring and Current Flow

you can repair fingers that are **almost** worn through by applying a drop of solder to the top part of the curved portion of the fingers.

The usual problem with fingers that do not conduct is that they have lost their spring. To remedy this problem remove the finger set by twisting the metal prongs on each end of the unit and slide the finger board up and off. With small tweezers (not pliers) carefully bend the fingers down. If the drum is still dirty, polish it with a Q-tip and solvent. Replace the finger unit and observe it to see if there is now enough spring in the fingers to make contact with the drum. Make the same check and adjustment for the lower fingers.

If the wires are missing or if you cannot find the ends that connect with the plug, you will have to replace the wires completely. The original wire was a very limp, stranded material that is frequently difficult to find. A good substitute is phonograph tone-arm pickup wire that you can get at a local radio-TV store. Or, you can use telephone receiver wire. In either case, remove all the heavy outer insulation and use only the inner insulated wires. The use of any other, heavier wire will not work. It will pull the tender off the track if it is too stiff.

Now for the moment of truth! Before you put the body back on the tender chassis connect the wires to the engine. The reverse unit should go through its cycle smoothly. If not, try some more TV contact cleaner. If the engine does not run, it is probably a problem with the motor.

If the engine runs replace the tender body. Leave enough wire to extend to the engine. Replace the drawbar and try the locomotive on a piece of test track which includes a half circle of curved track. The curved section will allow you to determine whether the wire alignment between the tender and the engine is correct. If there is too little wire or if the wire is too stiff, the engine will lift the tender off the track and stop the train.

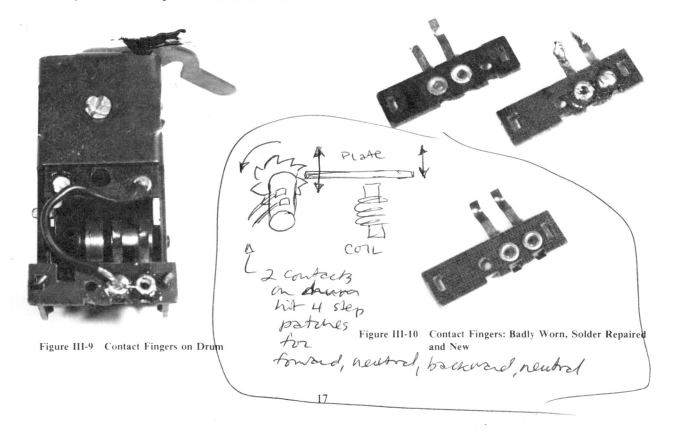

Figure III-9   Contact Fingers on Drum

Figure III-10   Contact Fingers: Badly Worn, Solder Repaired and New

17

MODIFIED OPERATION

If you want to **eliminate** all sources of reverse unit problems, you can eliminate the reverse unit altogether! The series wound universal motors that were used in all Gilbert-AF engines operate on both alternating (AC) and direct (DC) current. If you use DC, you can remove the reverse unit and replace it with a diode bridge.

Gilbert actually tried to introduce DC trains in the early days of S Gauge (1947), but due to poor market acceptance, they abandoned the project in 1950. The marketing problem concerned the materials available for motors. Alnico magnet material was still in its early stages of development.

A major stumbling block to DC operation in the late 1940s was the lack of an inexpensive method of converting AC (house current) to the 15 volts direct current necessary to operate the trains. Gilbert tried state-of-the-art electronic designs with its #14 rectiformer. The tube was designed by Sylvania (#x6089) and improved in 1949 (#1237). This $25

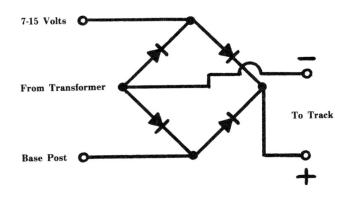

Figure III-11 Diagram for Converting AC Transformer to DC Operation
Most Bridge Rectifiers have leads marked for AC in, (+) and out (-).

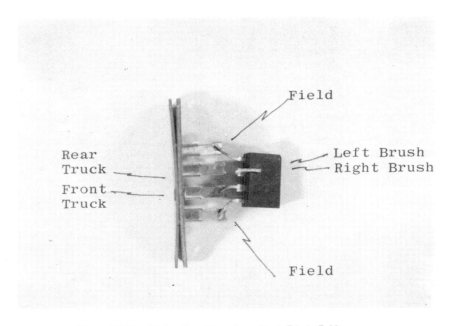

Figure III-12 Wiring For Reversing with A Diode Bridge
Wires come from pickups in the tender or from trucks in the diesel. The rear pickup goes to the left brush and the front pickup goes to the third bridge lead. The field wires go to the two outside bridge leads and the second bridge lead goes to the right brush. By reversing the field connections you can change the direction of the engine relative to the other engines.

18

thyratron device was more expensive than the most costly AC transformer and only produced 150 watts. Gilbert also made a rectifier with a four amp capacity that could be connected between the regular AC transformer and the track to produce direct current. This device was rather bulky and cost $12.95, a lot of money in those days.

Today, in a modern electronics store, you can buy a small, inexpensive six amp full wave rectifier bridge that makes DC operation from your present AF transformer easy. Radio Shack offers such a solid state device for less than $2 (#276-1180). It comes complete with hookup instructions. All you need to add is a double pole, double throw switch to act as the reversing device. Figure III-11 shows the wiring diagram for converting any AC train transformer to DC operation. If you want to make full use of the DC operation by removing the reverse unit, use a bridge rectifier such as the four amp #276-1146 Radio Shack device. The connection to the motor is quite easy. You will need only two wires leading from the tender pickups to the engine. The rear truck lead goes to the left brush. The front truck lead goes to one of the inner bridge leads. The other brush is connected with the other inner bridge lead. The field is connected to the outer bridge leads. Figure III-12 shows a picture of the connections, and III-13 is a schematic diagram.

With the conversion to direct current operation you will find that your trains run smoother and more reliably.

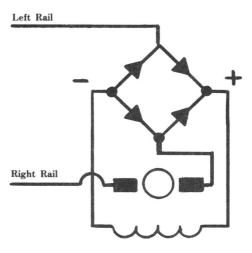

Figure III-13 Diagram for Bridge Rectifier
How to connect a Bridge Rectifier to a universal series motor for direct current operation.

Chapter IV
SERVICING STEAM ENGINES

After the job we did on the tender and reverse unit in the last chapter, we will assume that all is "go" with the power pickup and concentrate on the heart of the drive train—the worm drive motor.

Since the K-5 is one of my favorite engines and has sufficient side rod detail to make it representative of the more complex engines, we will use it as our example.

The first thing to ask yourself before you begin to disassemble the entire engine is, "does the engine really need to be taken apart?" If it runs but not as powerfully as you would like, then cleaning the commutator slots may be all that is necessary. To do this, turn the engine and tender over and place them in your engine holder to prevent scratching. Connect the alligator clips from your test track transformer to the tender wheels as shown in Figure IV-1. Since the reverse unit is activated by gravity, manually move the locking lever on the bottom of the tender to get the motor to run. Using the directing pipe supplied with the TV contact spray, direct a stream of cleaner on the rotating commutator. You will probably notice a sudden increase in speed and a reduction of current flow on you ammeter. Now stop the engine and mop up the excess cleaner and dirt with a Q-tip. Dirt was causing the engine to slow down. With a straight pin, scrape out the accumulated dirt in the three slots of the commutator. If the commutator is only moderately dirty, the TV contact spray will clean it and you will not need to disassemble the engine.

Disassembly

If you decide that it is necessary to disassemble the engine, start with the three valve gear screws on each side of the engine, shown in Figure IV-2. Notice that screw #1 is different from screws #2 and #3. Remove the screw that holds the piston slider to the boiler. Detach the tender and turn the engine over. Take the pilot wheels, piston and chassis apart by removing the screws in the bottom of the engine. Be sure that the smokestack is unscrewed before you separate the chassis from the boiler.

Now unscrew the jack panel at the rear of the engine cab and unsolder the headlamp at the front. You should be able to slide the chassis away from the body. Slide it forward and lift it out from the rear of the boiler. Do not attempt to pull the chassis right out or you will break off the holding tabs that are located about one-third of the way from the rear of the engine.

To remove the brushes, place your thumb over the brush housing end and slowly pull the brush cap off. Slowly release your thumb allowing the brush spring to extend. Do not let the brush spring off too quickly or it will fly across the room! Do the same with the other brush and then remove the springs. Leave the brushes in place for now and unscrew the two long screws that hold the rear brush-holder assembly to the rest of the motor. Now push the brushes out with one of the long screws and clean them in solvent. Clean the brush tubes and the entire brush housing. Check the length of the brushes. They should be 3/16 of an inch long. If not, replace them.

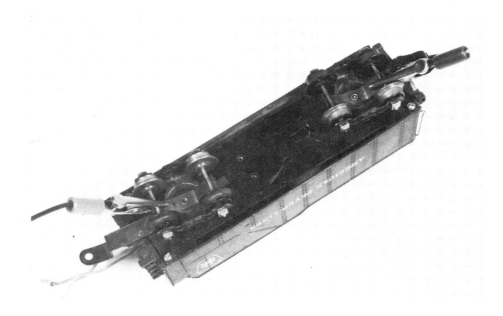

Figure IV-1   Alligator Clip Connection to Tender Wheels

Disassemble the rest of the motor by sliding the field off the two pins that are a part of the chassis casting. Remove the armature by unscewing it from the worm gear. Clean these parts with solvent. Clean the commutator slots with a pin and, if necessary, polish the commutator with super fine (#400) sandpaper. If the commutator is pitted and worn, it could indicate that the armature has been thrust up against the brush tubes. If this is the case, you probably noticed slow running in the forward direction. If the wear is excessive, you will have to replace the armature and upon reassembly check the alignment of the commutator with the brush tubes.

Figure IV-2   Side Rod Detail, K-5

Review the specifications listed for motors in the "Round-house Records"—check resistance, brush spring lengths (you can stretch springs to the proper length) and alignments.

Figure IV-3   Loose Tire Shorting Through Switch

One item on the checklist describes a problem that plagues a great number of engines: engine shorting through switches. Figure IV-3 shows an engine with loose tires going through a switch. Figure IV-4 shows the loose tires that cause the short circuit that stops the engine. These outer tires are made of metal, as are tires on real engines, but when AF tires come loose, they brush up against the chassis and cause a short. Figure IV-5 shows the three-piece sandwich of the metal

Figure IV-4   Loose Tire, Underside

wheel, the plastic insulator and outside metal tire that makes up the drive wheels on most AF steam engines. (Some later engines had all plastic wheels or plastic wheels with metal tires.)

Figure IV-5   Three-part Steam Engine Drive Wheel: Core, Insulator and Tire

If you have a loose tire, you can pull the wheel with your wheel puller and repair it, or you can leave it on the engine and use an epoxy putty to tighten the tire. Figure IV-6 shows the putty, which has been formed into a thin strip, being squeezed into the space between the insulator and the outer tire, where most breaks take place. Before applying the putty clean out any oil or grease. The putty works well since it does not run, adds bulk and holds the parts together. The cause of the loose wheel is usually a shrinking of the plastic insulator.

If you do remove the wheel from the chassis to repair it, use your wheel puller. Remove the side rods with a nut driver. Place the two jaws of the wheel puller (see Chapter I on Tools and Parts) next to the chassis and under the wheel to be pulled. You will have to first open up the jaws and extend the center screw. Now, align the center screw to the axle point in the center of the wheel and screw it until the wheel is pulled off the axle, as shown in Figure IV-7.

Take the wheel apart and clean off any dirt or oily residue with solvent. Use the epoxy putty to fix the wheel if necessary. Replacing the wheel or wheels on the engine must

Figure IV-6   Wheel Repair Using Epoxy Putty

be done carefully or the side rods will bind and the engine will not move. Gilbert manufactured a tool, the R-2, for this purpose and a few are still being sold—Dan Olson is one person who has advertised the R-2 tool for sale. (See Appendix to this Chapter for R-2 Tool Kit Instructions.) In replacing the wheels the object is to align the drive wheels so that the stud nuts, which hold the side rods, are in a perfect row on each side of the engine. The trick is to line them up on one side and then line them up on the other side. To complicate matters, the wheels are "quartered" or set a quarter of a turn ahead from one side of the chassis to the other. Figure IV-8 shows the proper alignment. The quartering requires patience. It also helps if you replace the driver connected to the worm gear first and then use it to align the other drive wheels. Start with the right side of the engine as seen from the cab and replace the wheels. You should use finger pressure to squeeze them on initially, then a vise to press them home. If the wheel goes on too easily it will slip,

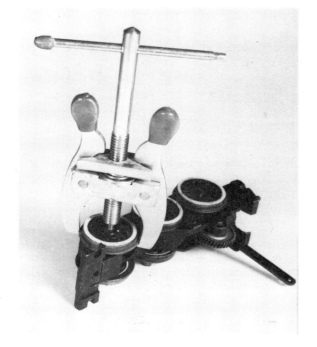

Figure IV-7   Using A Wheel Puller

and the wheel or the axle or both should be replaced. If you do not have a quartering tool, align the replacement wheels with the side rod and make sure they are set with the side rod at the bottom of the wheel as shown in Figure IV-9. Turn the engine over on its other side making sure that nothing moves. Position each driver on the left side so it is 90 degrees or a quarter turn ahead of the studs on the other side. Again, start with the driver attached to the worm gear and align the others with it. You may find it necessary to make slight adjustments in the alignment until the proper quartering is accomplished. You will quickly know when the alignment is faulty because the engine will stall and the side rods will bind. If you have an R-2, the tool's instructions explain its use and you should have no difficulty in quartering the wheels. From our discussion of quartering, you have probably concluded that it is better to fix the faulty tire while the wheel is on the engine!

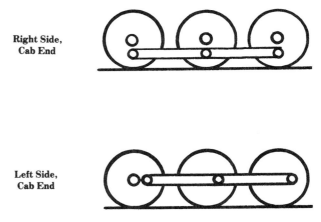

Right Side, Cab End

Left Side, Cab End

Figure IV-8   Quartering Steam Engine Drive Wheels

Smoke Clouds

Since most "steamers" can puff voluminous quantities of smoke, you will want to tune this feature while the engine is apart. Then the neighborhood kids will sit spellbound as you fill the air with rich, thick white clouds.

A number of "gremlins" can prevent smoke from pouring forth. The simplest to diagnose is fluid evaporation. If filling the chamber does not result in smoke billows, you might try loosening the wadded wick with an injection of non-flammable solvent. The solvent will be absorbed into the wick and allow it to work again. If the solvent does not free the wick, you should wait a few minutes before deciding on your next move. It may then be necessary to disassemble the smoke unit and rewind a new wick. Before you do this, check the chamber between the choo-choo cylinder and the smoke generator. It could be clogged. I once found a spider in this small place! If the smoke wisps out in light puffs rather than in synchronization with the choo-choo, then a blocked chamber is probably your problem. Use a pin to open the hole and unclog the chamber.

If there is still no smoke, disassemble the smoke unit by removing the screws that hold the smoke unit to the chassis. There are usually two screws, but on some later models there is only one screw to hold the unit on the chassis. Now unscrew the pilot light (#1449 bulb) and unsolder the two wires from the smoke unit that come from the back of the engine. You may think that it would be easier to replace the entire smoke unit. It may be, but someday you will run out of replacement parts and you may not know how to restore what you have. Besides, the job is not that difficult.

Figure IV-9   Using A Vise to Press On Wheels

With the unit detached, make a resistance check. You should read 35-50 ohms on the X1 scale of your VOM. If you get no reading, then the nichrome heating wire is burned out. To replace it, you will need about seven inches of #40 nickel chromium wire which can be purchased from the Magnet Wire Co. in New York City. However, the minimum length the Company sells is over a mile long and costs over $30. If you need to rewind a unit I can supply you with a length of the wire if you send your request with an envelope and stamp.

Remove the six screws on the top plate of the unit and carefully raise the wick-heater assembly. You will probably notice that the wick is badly hardened and burned. The heating wire is also probably broken at the solder connection. Pull the entire wick out. In earlier designs, four screws hold the lower chamber coverplate. Remove them to uncover the lower chamber. If the wick is very hard, it will not function and must be replaced. "Angel Hair," a Christmas fiberglass decoration, is a perfrect substitute for the horse hair used in the original wicks.

Use the old wick as a pattern for the new one. Since the #40 nichrome wire has a resistance of 70 ohms per foot, you will need from five to seven inches to obtain the 35 to 50 ohms specification. Do not use more wire or it will not get hot enough to vaporize the fluid. If you use too little, the wick will burn out prematurely.

To wind the coil, use a small wire brad (nail) as a form for the wick, as shown in Figure IV-10. Be sure that there is no overlap in the coil windings or the wire will burn out. When you have four to five inches of wire coiled, slide the nail out and tighten the coil at both ends of the wick. Now get the solder on the coverplate good and hot and slip the free ends of the coil you have just wound through the holes in the cover

from the underside. You can pull the fine #40 wire through with your tweezers. The nichrome wire cannot be soldered, so wind the protruding wires around the solder lugs on the top of the coverplate to get a good electrical connection.

Test for resistance at this point. If it measures over 50 ohms, you have too much wire on your coil. If you are below 30 ohms, you have too few turns on the coil or the windings have overlapped and the wick will burn out prematurely. The proper range is from 35 to 50 ohms.

If the resistance checks out, you are ready to put the wick back in the smoke unit. In the newer units you can easily stuff the wick into the cavity. In the older units, you will have to thread each end of the wick into a small hole and down into the lower chamber. If you moisten the wick with some smoke fluid before you thread it into the holes, the task is a bit easier. Once the wick is properly stowed away, just screw the chamber cover(s) down. Make sure that you do not allow the heating element wire to touch the chamber walls or to be bent in the process.

Make a final resistance check. Then check that the wire does not touch the metal portion of the smoke unit by placing one probe of your VOM on the smoke unit and touching the other probe to each of the coverplate solder lugs. When making these resistance checks, the smoke unit must be electrically isolated from any other part of the engine. If everything checks out, you can expect to see rich billows of smoke emerging from your engine.

During the first two years of AF S Gauge production, smoke units were not located in the boiler, but in the tender with their own worm drive motors and smoke generators that were connected to the smoke stack with a long length of rubber hose. Although smaller than boiler-mounted motors, tender motors are just the same as their big brothers and require the same service.

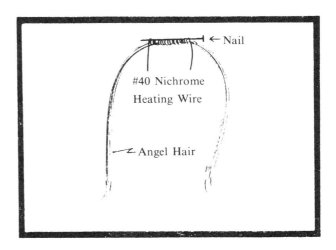

Figure IV-10   Wick Winding for A Smoke Unit

Clean up any oily residue and remove all caked grease. If your unit has the rubberized, cloth choo-choo generator, you will probably find that it is cracked and torn. Unscrew the entire smoke unit from the tender and stretch out the choo-choo bellows. Clean off any oil and apply a **thin** coating of "Duro Plastic Rubber" to seal the cracks. The cloth bellows is the only difference in this smoke unit, and you may not even have to repair it, since the factory issued a replacement part (that resembles the piston type used in the later choo-choo units). If the wick is burned out follow the procedure outlined above for its repair or replacement.

If you followed these procedures and made the repairs necessary, you should make a final check of the engine before putting the boiler casting back on the chassis.

To reassemble the motor put the field onto the chassis. Next screw the armature into the worm gears. Make sure that there is at least one washer on the worm end of the armature. Now put the brush housing back on the field. The bump on this housing should be on the bottom and not on the top. Insert the two long screws and snug them up to hold the motor to the chassis. Check for play and for interference between the brush tubes and the commutator. If the commutator rubs against the brush tubes, place a washer on the commutator end of the armature.

Next slide the brushes down the tubes and put the brush springs in after them, compress the springs with your thumb and slide the caps over the ends of the brush tubes. Use a few drops of oil on the wick at the rear of the motor and then squeeze out the excess. Do not over-oil since excess oil on the commutator can stop the flow of electricity.

Your engine's motor and smoke overhaul is now complete. If any of the checklist items did not meet specifications, you should have adjusted or replaced them. If you need to replace an armature, be sure that you get the correct configuration. Use a pull-mor armature from a pull-mor motor. If you use a pull-mor armature from a pre-pull-mor motor your engine will experience excessive current flow and slow operation. Figure IV-11 shows the two armatures. Note that the pull-mor armature has more closely spaced armature poles than the more open earlier design. If you need to rewind an armature or a field, we will cover that subject in Chapter VI.

Figure IV-11 Armature Differences Between Pre-Pull Mor and Pull Mor Motors

INSTRUCTIONS FOR USE OF WHEEL ALIGNMENT R-2 TOOL KIT

1. Remove defective drive wheels. If drive gear or chassis is defective, it should also be replaced. When replacing the worm gear, the axle should be inserted from the righthand side of the motor because of the oversized hole in the chassis and the oversized axle end.

2. Insert two flanged wheels and one flangeless wheel and stud in Tool #1, with the flangeless wheel and stud in the center. The thin pin on the die should be inserted in the threaded hole on the drive wheel.

3. Drive on a plain axle in the two drive wheels in the two front positions leaving the third one available for the worm gear axle.

4. The chassis assembly is assembled to the drive wheels in Tool #1 by driving down gear axle in plain flanged wheel.

5. The next step is to insert two flanged wheels and one flangeless wheel and stud in Tool #2, with the flangeless wheel and stud in the center.

6. Place Tool #1 with drive wheels on top of the axles and tap the top of Tool #2 a few times, so it will be held temporarily in place.

7. Insert the two tools and chassis assembly in a vise with the chassis upside down and then tighten the vise. Be sure that you have enough clearance between the wheel and chassis so that it is not too tight or too loose.

8. Remove chassis assembly from vise and tap off Tools #1 and #2 from drive wheels.

TOOL No. 1   TOOL No. 2

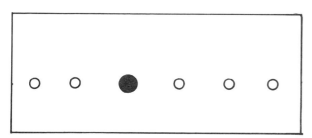

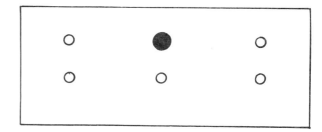

Chapter V
ALCO PA-1s AND GP-7s

Diesels seem to be more wear-prone than steam brutes.

First, the plastic bodies of the GP-7s and Alco diesels are fragile. Be sure to use an engine holder to support the engine when you remove the truck sides. There are two screws on each truck underside that will allow you to remove the cast sides. With these off, you will be able to reach to screws that hold the chassis to the body. There is provision for seven screws in an Alco but usually only five of these are used. Two screws hold the GP-7 body to the chassis. The "Geep" body comes off readily, but you will have to pull the chassis out of the Alco body since it is a tight fit. Put the body in a safe place, away from solvents, paint or a long drop to the floor!

Try the chassis mechanism on your test track. If it operates spasmodically, its pickup wheels may need to be cleaned of accumulated dirt and oil residue. Then adjust and clean the reverse unit as described in Chapter III. The heart of most diesel problems is the double-ended worm drive motor. The motor is the same for Alcos and Geeps, so follow these steps for both.

To get the motor assembly off the chassis either remove the retaining ring on top of the chassis motor pivot point as found on the older pre-1953 engines or spread the holder yoke over the screws at the bottom of the motor casting as on the newer models. On the latter, the motor will simply drop off the yoke.

Figure V-1   Dirty Diesel Chassis

Figure V-1 shows a motor's usual accumulation of grimy grease, dust and oil. Oil and grease are fine on bearings, but play havoc with electrical contacts like the commutator. As with the steam engines, it is possible to clean a diesel motor without its disassembly. Use a squirt of TV contact spray on the commutator and brushes, then a Q-tip to remove any grime. Diesel motors are more open than those of steam engines and are therefore more prone to dirt accumulation.

If you decide that it is necessary to disassemble the motor, start with the worm covers at either end of the motor. Next, remove the brass bearing strap by taking out the small screws on the side of the field opposite the brushes. The brush assembly and bearing strap are held down by two similar screws and should now be removed.

To reach the field, remove the yoke by first backing off the field adjusting screws located at the top of the yoke. One turn

Figure V-2   Proper Axle Seating for Diesel Drive Wheels

of each of these screws is all that is necessary. When the field is loose, remove the retaining screws at the bottom of the yoke to free the field. Clean all parts, including the chassis casting, in solvent. The caked grease acts like putty and causes excess drag on the motor which slows down the train.

Before discussing (in Chapter VI), a cure for a major cause of diesel failure, we will learn how to identify and understand its cause. The bushings for the axles of the diesel drive wheels are drilled into soft castings. Since the wheels pick up the current and are made of steel, these bushings wear both mechanically and electrically. If the bushings are oval rather than round, the wheels will wobble and bind. This can cause the engine to stall or run hot and slow. If your engine acts this way and the wobble is excessive, more than 3/32 of an inch, then use the procedure described in the next chapter to repair the chassis bushings or to replace the chassis. If you replace the chassis, do not throw away the old one. Save it for future repairs; such parts are almost extinct.

You will have to remove the wheels to replace or repair the chassis bushings. Use the wheel puller to get the wheels off as you did in Chapter IV when we serviced steam engines. Notice that since diesel wheels are designed to pick up current, there is a wheel with a plastic core and a wheel with a solid core. Remember the side each of these wheels is on by making a diagram of the chassis before you remove the wheels. If you mix up the wheels you can cause a direct short or stop all current going to the motor.

The next item to notice is that the axle is not symmetrical. One side of the casting has a slightly larger hole than the other side to allow the splined axle to slide in and out without scoring the bushing hole. When you drive the axle out of the bushings and remove the worm gear, note that the larger hole must be on the bottom. If you reverse the position the axle will become stuck and will not drive out. If the axle is forced out, the bushing holes could become enlarged or the worm gear shattered.

After repairing the chassis, reverse the wheel pulling process. First insert the worm gear and drive the axle in place, through the hole. Consult your diagram of the chassis and finger press the wheels back in place. Then use a vise to snug them up. The ends of the axle should extend just beyond the wheels as shown in Figure V-2 to assure the correct gauging of the drivers. A piece of track can also be used to check on this specification. There should be some play from front to back so that the drivers do not bind on the curves and jump the tracks.

After the wheels are aligned, slide the armature assembly into the field with the field connection wires on the brush side of the armature, as shown in Figure V-3. Replace the bearing strap on the end away from the commutator. If the screw holes have become enlarged, use a longer screw to get the strap tight. It must be held down securely to prevent play and poor operation.

Figure V-3   Diesel Brush Position

On the brush end, start a screw into the hole and put the bearing strap and brush holder under it. Fasten this side loosely. Put the other screw through the brush holder and strap. Screw both screws almost tight. Position the brushes with the brush springs in place so that the brushes ride close to the center of the commutator and are perpendicular to it.

The last reassembly adjustment is critical to the engine's proper operation. Slip the field yoke over the bottom of the casting. The field should be loose. If it is not, then unscrew the centering (set) screws on the top of the yoke and adjust the centering of the field over the armature.

After tightening the set screws and all other screws, try out the engine. Do this off the track by attaching the power leads to the solder points at the top of each truck and holding the motor up, out of contact with any surface. Run the motor forward and in reverse. Check that the armature does not touch the field. If it does, the engine will stop or slow down to a crawl. To correct, loosen the centering set screws on the side of the yoke where the field touches the armature and tighted up the other side. The armature must be centered for proper operation.

If you find it impossible to keep the armature centered when the engine is powered make sure that the bearing straps are holding the armature shaft snug. Or, worn armature bearings may need to be replaced. To remove these bearings you will have to drive the armature shaft off the worm. This can be done, as shown in Figure V-4, with a nail set. Solder the worm back on the shaft end after the bearings are replaced.

After all adjustments have been made, place a small amount of Libriplate (or other light grease) on the gears and a drop of oil on the armature bearings. Keep in mind that

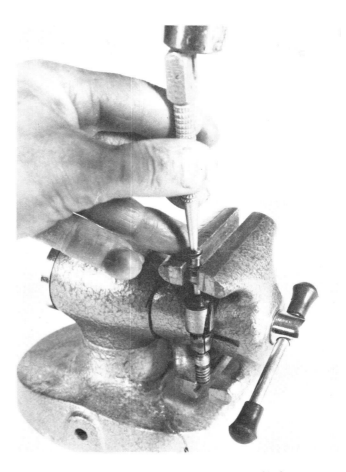

Figure V-4   Driving Worm Off Armature Shaft

excess oil can adversely affect the electrical system. Therefore, wipe away any excess oil. Try the drive assembly before you replace the diesel body. If it runs well, replace the body and truck sides. It should continue to run smoothly for many hours before needing another overhaul in your roundhouse.

Chapter VI
MAJOR ENGINE OVERHAULS

Now that we have covered engine disassembly and diagnosed some of the major causes of AF engine failure, we will address two major problem areas that stop our trains from running: shorted or burned out motors and worn out diesel bushings. While these are major in scope, fortunately, they do not occur too often.

Our solution for shorted or burned out motors applies to steam engines as well as diesels. While fields and armatures for steam-type locomotives are still in good supply, I would suggest that you begin practicing how to rewind them since the supply will not last forever. To find a diesel field or armature these days is a rare event, so if one burns out, you will have to rewind it.

To rewind a motor you need a spool of the proper enameled wire (available at Radio Shack or Lafayette Radio stores) and some patience. The following Table gives wire gauges and lengths for the common steam and diesel fields and armatures.

Table VI - 1

Field and Armature Wire Gauges and Lengths

Application	Wire Gauge	Length Needed
Steam Fields	#24	40 Feet
Steam Armatures	#26	Three 11 Foot Pieces
Diesel Fields	#26	35 Feet
Diesel Armatures	#30	Three 7½ Foot Pieces

If you have an engine that does not fit into one of these categories and you do not know its gauge, send me a one-inch piece of the wire and I will measure it for you. (Be sure to include a stamped, self-addressed envelope with your request.)

Winding Fields

The best way to learn how to wind a field is to unwind the defective one and observe how the factory wound it. You will note that the windings follow a tight pattern. You can visualize the way a field is wound if you think of the way a level-wound fishing reel lays the line on the spool. There should not be any criss-crossed windings. A uniform winding will provide the proper electromagnetic force.

A good field should have a cold DC-resistance of 1 to 2 ohms. A measurement in this range is subject to variation, so make sure that your meter is properly set to zero. Fields usually do not burn out. The main reason why they need to be rewound is that an inner wire breaks off, as shown in Figure VI-1.

After taking off and disposing of the old wire, measure a new length and leave an extra three inch piece extending outside of the core's center. Carefully wind the field until you have used up all the wire. If you cannot wind it all on the core without its bulging out, cut off the wire after at least seventy-five percent is wound around the core. If you wind on less it would be best to start over again, making sure that you pull the wire tightly on each turn.

Winding Armatures

Figure VI-1   Broken Field Wire (circled)

Armatures are more likely to burn out because they are made with a finer gauge wire. You should have a 1 to 2 ohms cold DC-resistance between any adjacent positions on the commutator. If the resistance is higher, the winding is open. Examine the outside of the winding for a break in the wire, where it is more likely to occur. Remove turns of the wire until you come to the break and reconnect the end to the commutator. This saves a lot of time and effort. There are two possibilities:
  (1) the break is visible on the outside. In this case unwind several turns to reach it and to provide enough wire for resoldering.
  (2) the break is most likely not visible on the outside. Hopefully, you will find it by removing only four or five turns. If you have to remove more than five turns to locate the break you should probably either add a short length of wire to compensate for the lost length or rewire the entire wiring.

If the resistance reads zero, the winding has shorted out and will have to be replaced. A short circuit usually indicates that the armature was subjected to excessive current. If the resistance still reads zero after the wire is replaced be sure to look for the cause of the trouble before burning out another armature.

Start repairing the burned out armature by carefully unwinding the three coils. Note the direction (usually counterclockwise) of the windings, and where they connect to the commutator. Figure VI-2 shows the proper connections, but you must be very careful that the proper armature pole is connected to its commutator piece. I have made the mistake of putting the wire on one commutator piece too close to the armature pole and finding that the armature would not rotate. When you come to the end of the unwinding, you will see that the three wires are soldered together as a set. In making your new set of wires, scrape off the enamel from the wire ends and twist them in a pigtail so that they can be readily soldered. To assure that the armature field poles do not contact the pigtail, dip the pigtail in epoxy or Duco cement as an insulator.

You can start with any of the poles, but you must wind them carefully. Each pole must be wound in the same direction or the motor will refuse to turn. As you wind, make sure that the wire does not bulge away from the longer side of the pole (as it tends to) by pressing it in with a blunt instrument. If you cannot wind the full footage on a pole, you probably have too much bulge. If you wind on less than eighty percent of the wire, start over again. If you come within a foot of the length, you have wound it excellently! After all three poles are wound, connect the free ends to the proper commutator pieces. As figure VI-2 shows, the correct commutator connection is the piece just ahead of the armature, not the one right next to it.

In general, the tighter and more uniform the windings, the smoother the operation. Take your time and do not be discouraged, it does take practice.

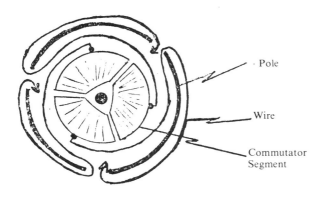

Figure VI-2   Pole Windings and Commutator Connections For A Typical Armature
All windings go in the same direction.

Worn Out Diesel Wheel and Axle Bushings

The second major overhaul problem concerns diesel wheel and axle bushings that have worn from a circular to an oval shape. The usual cause of this condition stems from friction between the hard steel axles and the soft zamak castings. Only in the first years of production were diesel bushings made of brass and their wear is noticeably less.

The basic idea in restoring a bushing is to drill out the old hole and implant a new brass bushing. Therefore, you will need a bushing, the proper drills and a drill press or drill stand. Do not attempt this job with a hand-held drill or the holes will not be straight and the chassis will have to be scrapped.

Replacement bushings are commercially available from your local bearing dealer. I recommend an "Oilite" bearing, #AA-238 bronze sleeve. It is the closest available in this line which can be drilled out to meet AF axle specifications. You will also need #14 and #19 drill bits. To enlarge the hole use a ¼-inch drill bit. If you cannot find the bushings, I can purchase them for you locally. They cost about $1.50 each and two are needed to complete a rebushing of one chassis since they can be cut in half.

Replacing a Bushing

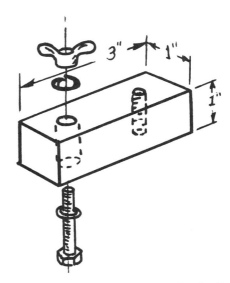

Figure VI-3   Chassis Mounting Jig For Diesel Bushing Repair

First, bore out the original axle hole with a ¼-inch drill bit. (You will have already removed all the other motor parts and cleaned the chassis.) Mount the chassis on the drill press with the larger hole of the chassis up. Mark this (up) side for future reference because diesel holes are not of the same size. Make sure that the chassis is held down securely before drilling. Figure VI-3 is a suggested jig for holding the chassis. Drill slowly into the soft metal and drill through both sides with one motion. Figure VI-4 shows the chassis being drilled with this jig.

After cleaning up the metal shavings, fit the oilite bushing into the holes. Place a drop of Loctite "Stud n' Bearing Mount" in the hole and then squeeze the bushing firmly into the hole with an arbor press or a vise, as shown in Figure VI-5. Press the bushing in only half way and wait ten minutes for the cement to cure. Then, very carefully cut the other half of the bushing off and press it into the other hole on the other side in the same way. File the rough, cut part of the bushing so that it is smooth and flush with the chassis side. The inside of the bushing will be smooth since the factory-finished end should be pressed in first.

Figure VI-4   Jig For Holding Diesel Chassis

Clear off any loose filings and remount the chassis on your drill press. Align the bushing with the drill bit and make sure that you have the marked side—the side with the larger hole—up. Drill through both sides of the new bushing with a #19 drill bit. Change the bit to a #14 and without disturbing the set-up, drill **only** the top side hole with a #14 bit. Use very sharp, unworn bits when drilling out the oilite bearings. Repeat the process for and diesel wheels that have excessive wobble. Replace the axle, worm gear and wheels as described in Chapter V. Be sure to insert the axle in the proper direction so you do not enlarge the smaller hole.

Figure VI-6   Pressing Bushing Into Chassis

Figure VI-5   Chassis Being Drilled Using A Jig

Chapter VII
WHISTLES AND HORNS

Figure VII-1   314AW Whistle Assembly

What's a railroad without a lonesome whistle wailing down the track? The Gilbert AF engineers knew the importance of this whistle and designed a variety of external whistles and a horn that was incorporated into a rolling stock. The externally-mounted whistle was usually disguised as a billboard! The mechanism itself could also be purchased as an Erector whistle for use with A.C. Gilbert & Co. toys.

The whistle is quite simple. Its universal motor provides the power for a small impeller fan which blows air into a sound chamber to create the whistle sound. There are usually two exit chambers on the whistle which produce a pleasing sound. In the "two-in-one" whistle, there is a baffle plate over one of the exit chambers. By pushing the control button, the baffle is moved by a solenoid and the sound changes.

To keep a blower-type whistle in "sound shape," follow the procedure outlined for servicing motors under steam engines. It is the **same** motor found in your engine, the only difference being that it rotates only in one direction. This brings us to a possible problem you may experience with blower whistles. If the motor rotates in the wrong direction, the blower does not blow air but sucks it through the chambers. It also produces a very weak, sometimes non-existent, sound. To remedy this problem reverse the brush connections and thereby reverse the motor's direction. Now the blower will **blow** air through the whistle.

Let us review the steps to bring the blower motor up to proper operation: clean the commutator and slots; place a small amount of oil on the rear armature bushing; make sure that the brushes are clean and of sufficient length—3/16 of an inch.

Another cause of whistle failure is a disintegrated impeller. It disintegrates because it spins at such a high speed. In this case you can sometimes patch the problem up by gluing together the pieces you find in the blower housing. Use your cyanoacrylate cement (Eastman 910) to put the pieces together.

A first cousin to the billboard whistle is the tender-mounted version found in the PRR K-5 314AW. Its system, actually a copy of Lionel's, was judged to infringe on the Lionel patent, so it was produced for only a short time. This is

unfortunate, since it was the only steam-type whistle that sounded real. This whistle worked in an ingenious way. The concept was to impose a DC voltage on top of the AC voltage used to operate the train. There is a small DC-activated relay in the engine's tender which turns the whistle motor on while the engine races down the track. It is a small version of the billboard-type whistle. Figure VII-1 pictures the relay, whistle and reverse unit, all crammed into the tender!

To activate the whistle, you need a momentary source of DC power. Figure VII-2 is a diagram for you to use to build your own circuit. The Gilbert control had no number, but looked like a number 1½ transformer. The wiring diagram for this control is at the end of this chapter along with instructions on how to hook up the other types of whistles to the track.

In the circuit in Figure VII-2, the diode provides the DC power and the 500 mfd capacitor allows a small flow of AC current to keep the engine running without slowing down. If you choose to run your engine on direct current, you will not be able to use the 314AW since the DC source will continually energize the whistle relay.

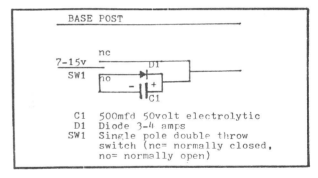

Figure VII-2   314AW Whistle Control Box

The adjustment of the return spring (shown in Figure VII-3) is critical to the proper operation of the 314AW whistle. If the tension is too great, the solenoid will not pull the switch into

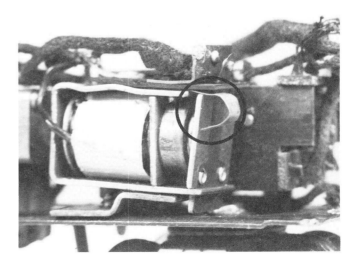

Figure VII-3   314AW Return Spring (circled)

contact; but if the tension is insufficient, the whistle will not kick-out when the DC pulse is removed. You can stretch, shorten or replace the spring to make it operate smoothly, although some patience is helpful in this trial and error process.

The whistle motor is serviced in the same way as is the billboard motor. I've found that to get the best sound from a 314AW, you will have to run your engine almost wide open, at 12 to 15 volts, or else the whistle sounds quite sick.

In 1950 AF introduced an electronic whistle. A.C. Gilbert was always experimenting with the latest in electrical and electronic gadgetry and this innovation was a logical extension of that research. As Figure VII-4 shows, the

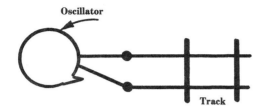

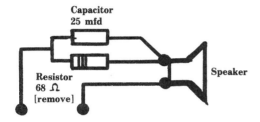

Figure VII-4   Electronic Whistle Schematic

concept for the electronic whistle involves an oscillator and a speaker. The oscillator fed the track with a 600 cycles per second sound which was picked up by the engine or tender wheels and sent into the speaker. Since the alternating current was also oscillating, the speaker continually picked up the 60 cycles per second "buzz," and a filter capacitor was therefore wired in series with the speaker. Since the early oscillators did not produce loud sounds, there will sometimes be found a 68 ohm resistor in parallel with the capacitor. It was placed there to increase the sound flow to the speaker. Unfortunately, all it seems to do is heat up and in some plastic shell engines, I have seen evidence of melting from this resistor's heat. For this reason, I suggest that you cut one of the connections on the resistor to remove it from the circuit. With the newer whistle generators there is not a noticeable difference in the quality of sound after this destructive resistor is removed.

The small speaker used in an engine or tender sometimes burns out and must be replaced. Finding a miniature speaker can be a problem, but you should be able to pick up one for about $2 to $3 from Radio Shack. They are usually designed for transistor radios and have a 3.2 ohm rating. Look for the speaker with the smallest diameter, from around one to one-and-a-half inches, to assure that it fits into the tender or engine.

To hook it up, connect one wire to the speaker and the capacitor to the other speaker terminal. Be careful not to apply too much heat or you can melt off the speaker terminals. Follow Figure VII-4 for the correct wiring. Use a 25 microfarad, 35 volt electrolytic capacitor. Polarity is not important in this AC system.

Figure VII-6   #710 Steam Whistle Control

There were two controllers for the "Air Chime" whistle. The first controller, made only in 1950, runs on 110 volts and is quite a complex electronic part. It is without a number and is usually called the "electronic whistle controller box." It was manufactured in small quantities, until the Korean War started when the lack of raw materials stopped production. The successor to this complex generator was more reliable and produced a louder sound.

If you have an "electronic whistle control box," and you wish it to sound forth loudly, replace the two electrolytic capacitors (C1 and C2). Figure VII-5 is a schematic wiring diagram of this device to help you locate these capacitors. Try to replace the capacitors with values as close to the originals as possible (+ or - 5 mfd) and at voltage ratings equal to or in excess of the originals. The tube, a 117P7, is still available, but costs over $9, so replace it as a last resort only. The Air Chime Whistle was redesigned in a steam and diesel configuration to replace the electronic control box. It was based on a mechanical vibrator which produced a 600 cycle sound. The vibrators were readily available in the 1950s since they were used to provide the high voltage needed in automobile radios. I doubt if they are now available because automobiles feature transistor radios.

Figure VII-6A   Four Versions of Vibrator Tubes

There are four versions of the vibrator whistle tube, although superficially they look alike. Number one is the most common Air Chime whistle; number two, a black cardboard "diesel horn," is wired the same as number one; number three is a faded red cardboard tube which says "steam whistle," but does not work in the 710 control and number four, a black "steam whistle generator." Number four is the only tube which works in the #710 controller. It and the other three are shown in Figure VII-6A.

The correct wiring is shown in Figure VII-7. If you cannot find a black tube you can rewire the one you have as shown in this schematic.

There are three control buttons for the Air Chime controller.

The #710 steam whistle controller gives the most pleasing sound of the three, and its diagram is found in Figure VII-6. When you use it, you can control the frequency of the sound and achieve a more realistic effect. While on the subject of how it sounds, let me say that none of the whistle sounds sound "real," although the catalogues say they do! The whistle in fact, sounds more like a buzzer than a horn or whistle.

If the generator tubes do not work, you can clean and adjust them. Cut the tube at the base to reach its inner workings. The "tube" is not a vacuum-type and does not suffer from being taken apart. The usual problem is dirty contacts on the vibrator. To clean them, use a fine #400 grit sandpaper. When finished, replace the protective shell and use epoxy or tape to hold it together.

If you are curious about how the value of the filter capacitor came about, the following formula and table will explain it. In an AC circuit, a capacitor acts something like a resistor and holds back a certain amount of electricity depending on the

Figure VII-5 110 Volt Electronic Whistle Circuit Diagram

C1   25 mfd, 25 volt Elec.
C2   40-20-25 mfd 150-150-50 volt elec.
C3, C6   .002 mfd 200 volt
C4, C5   .003 mfd 600 volt
R1   1600Ω 1 w
R2   100Ω 2 w
R3   3.6 MΩ 1w
R4   330 KΩ 1w
R5   330 KΩ 1w

R6   2MΩ pot.
R7   2MΩ pot.
X1   NE2
X2   NE2
V1   117P7
S1   SPDT spring loaded
T1   no marking
CH1   no marking

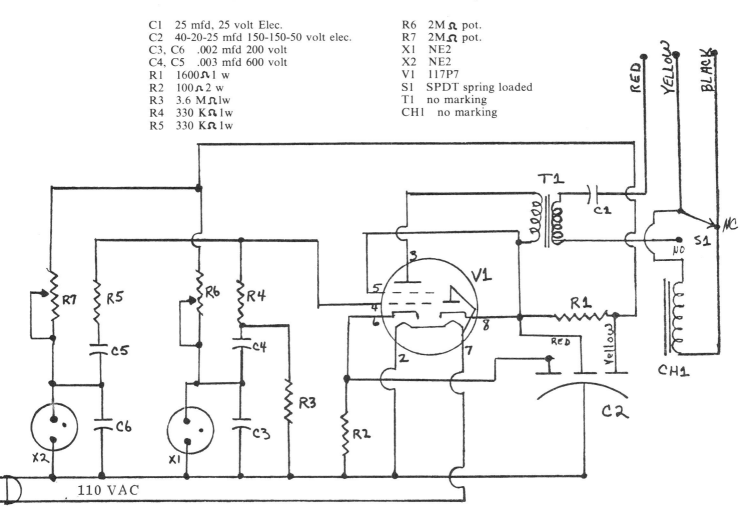

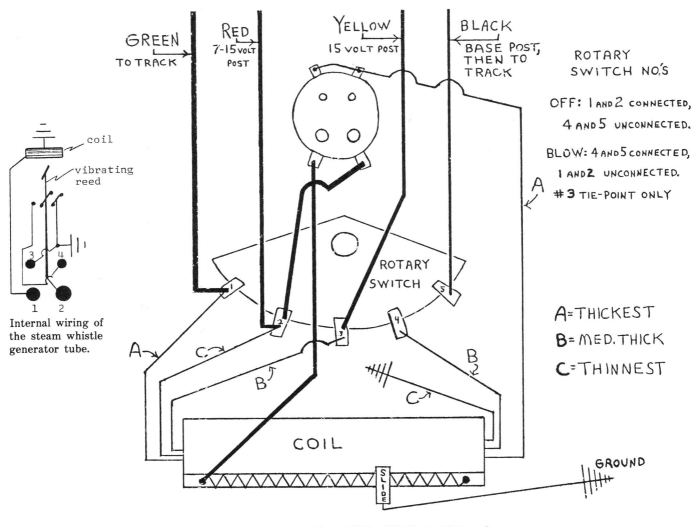

GREEN TO TRACK

RED 7-15 VOLT POST

YELLOW 15 VOLT POST

BLACK BASE POST, THEN TO TRACK

ROTARY SWITCH NO.'S

OFF: 1 AND 2 CONNECTED, 4 AND 5 UNCONNECTED.

BLOW: 4 AND 5 CONNECTED, 1 AND 2 UNCONNECTED.

#3 TIE-POINT ONLY

A = THICKEST
B = MED. THICK
C = THINNEST

coil
vibrating reed

3 4
1 2

Internal wiring of the steam whistle generator tube.

ROTARY SWITCH

COIL

SLIDE

GROUND

Figure VII-7   #710 Control Schematic

frequency of the AC and the capacitance of the capacitor. The resistance is called the "capacitive reactance" and is defined as:

$$X_c = \frac{1}{2\pi fc}$$

where π = 3.14159
  f = Frequency
  C = capacitance in farads (a microfarad is 10^{-6} farads)

Table VII-1 Filter Capacitor Values

If we solve the formula for various frequencies and capacitances we get the following values:

Frequency (cycles/second)	Capacitance (mfd)	X_c (ohms)
60	5	530
60	10	265
60	25*	106
200	5	159
200	10	79
200	25	31
600	5	53
600	10	27
600	25*	11

From this Table you can see that a 25 mfd capacitor with a fairly high (106) reactance to the 60 cycle AC and only 11 ohms to the 600 cycle horn sound is the logical choice. A higher value capacitor would cause a continual hum in the speaker and a lower value, while eliminating the hum would give a softer horn sound.

APPENDIX

NO. 315 PENNSYLVANIA K5 "WHISTLING" LOCOMOTIVE and TENDER

This locomotive is the standard Pennsylvania K5 locomotive with a built in choo-choo and smoke unit, but the tender has a built in whistle unit which allows the operator to blow long or short blasts or any number of blasts as the train is running or standing still.

The whistle is designed to be used with AC current only.

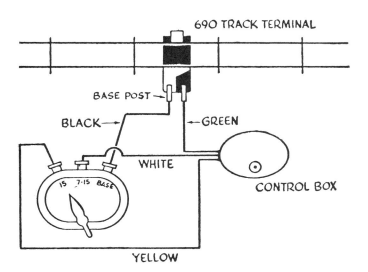

FIGURE VII-9
WHISTLE CONTROL BOX

The control box for the whistle is very simple to hook up.
1. Connect the **YELLOW WIRE** from the control box to the **15 VOLT POST** on the transformer.
2. Connect the **WHITE WIRE** from the control box to the **7-15 VOLT POST** on the transformer.
3. Connect the **GREEN WIRE** from the control box to the **RIGHT HAND CLIP** on the No. 690 track terminal.
4. Connect the separate **BLACK WIRE** between the **BASE POST** on the transformer and the **BASE POST CLIP** on the No. 690 track terminal.
NOTE: Be sure that no wire runs directly from the 7 to 15 volt post on the transformer to the track terminal.

If the control box is to be hooked into a layout which has already been wired, be sure any wires from the 7-15 volt post to the track are removed. Then proceed with the hook up as shown on the instruction sheet. In the case of extra feed or jumper wires to distant points on the track, be sure they are not hooked directly to the transformer but to the No. 690 track terminal.

The train should now be ready to operate. Place the locomotive and tender on the track and turn on the transformer. While the train is running, flip on the switch projecting from the top of the whistle control box. As long as the switch is held in contact the whistle will blow. The transformer handle should be turned on while blowing the whistle. If the transformer is turned off and the whistle is blown, the locomotive will be getting power causing it to run. Therefore, stop it in a neutral position with the transformer handle on to blow the whistle while train is standing.

OILING THE WHISTLE UNIT

To oil the whistle unit remove the four corner screws on the underneath side of the tender and remove the tender body, then place a small amount of fine oil on the oil wick at each end of the armature shaft. One wick is located on the top plate in front of the brush holder and the other wick is located in the cross frame at the rear of the armature.

ELECTRONIC WHISTLE CONTROL
HOOK UP INSTRUCTIONS

To install the electronic whistle control box, study the following diagrams and use the one which corresponds to the type of power source you have.

If you are using a transformer, see Figure VII-10

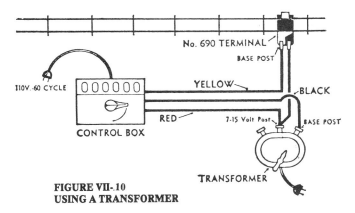

FIGURE VII-.10
USING A TRANSFORMER

1. Connect the **RED WIRE** from control box to the **7-15 VOLT POST** on the transformer.
2. Connect the **BLACK WIRE** from the control box to the **BASE POST** on the transformer.
3. Connect the **YELLOW WIRE** from the control box to the **BASE POST CLIP** on the No. 690 track terminal.
4. Connect a wire from the **7-15 VOLT POST** on the transformer to the other clip ont eh No. 690 track terminal.

If you are using a transformer and No. 15 Rectifier, see Figure VII-11

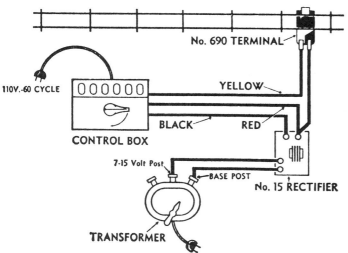

FIGURE VII-II
USING A TRANSFORMER
AND No. 15 RECTIFIER

1. Connect the **BLACK WIRE** from the control box to the **LEFT HAND DC POST** on the No. 15 rectifier.
2. Connect the **RED WIRE** from the control box to the **RIGHT HAND DC POST** on the No. 15 rectifier
3. Connect the **YELLOW WIRE** from the control box to the **BASE POST CLIP** on the No. 690 track terminal.
4. Connect a wire from the **RIGHT HAND POST** on the No. 15 rectifier to the **OTHER CLIP** on the No. 690 track terminal.

WIRING

1. Connect the **BLACK WIRE** from the control box to the **BASE POST** on the transformer.
2. Connect the **RED WIRE** from the control box to the **7-15 VOLT POST** on the transformer.
3. Connect the **YELLOW WIRE** from the control box to the **15 VOLT POST** on the transformer.
4. Connect the separate **BLACK WIRE** packed with the track terminal from the **BASE POST** on the transformer to the **BASE POST CLIP** on the 690 track terminal.
5. Connect the **GREEN WIRE** from the control box to the other clip on the 690 track terminal.

NOTE: Be sure no other wires run directly from the transformer to the track. If jumper or booster wires are to be used on large layouts to give an even flow of current, be sure wires are run from the No. 690 track terminal shown in the diagram to another track terminal. Do not run wires directly from the transformer to the track.

OPERATION

Next, place the generator on the control box, inserting the 4 prongs into the holes. There are two large and two small prongs which only fit into their respective holes. The whistle is now ready to operate; place the locomotive on the track, then turn the power on, press the control box button and the whistle should blow. If the whistle is to be blown while locomotive is standing still, the power should be on and the locomotive reverse control should be in neutral position.

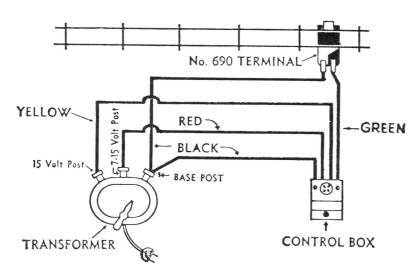

HOOKING UP AND OPERATING THE AIR CHIME WHISTLE CONTROL

FIRST, remove all wires which are now supplying current to the track for train operation. Disregard other wiring instructions received with the transformer or track terminal.

NEXT, study the following diagram and follow the instructions below. Only one track terminal is to be used and the **wires must be connected as shown** in the diagram.

Chapter VIII
ACCESSORIES

The Gilbert Plant produced an array of action accessories for American Flyer trains. Like the engines we have discussed, the accessories are simple machines, built from relatively uncomplicated mechanical parts and activated by simple eletrical devices, such as motors or solenoids. For example, a solenoid is a coil of wire wrapped around a magnetic core such as steel or iron. On accessories such as action cars, semaphores or loading platforms, the solenoid is wound around a hollow tube (core) and a plunger slides back and forth through the hollow tube. A return spring is usually used to move the plunger out of the tube. Return springs lose their strength from continual use and need to be stretched back into shape.

The following Figures show how to revitalize a return spring:

Of the motor activated accessories, only two, the coal loader and the electromagnetic crane, use the brush-type or universal motor, just like the ones found in steam engines. The crane has a four-step reversing unit and servicing it is identical to that for the engines we talked about in Chapter III (Reversing Units) and Chapter IV (Motors).

The motor for the coal loader has a special field for reversing. It consists of two separate windings which go in opposite directions. This was an ingenious way for Gilbert engineers to eliminate the reverse unit and still do the job. If you have to rewind a double-winding field, remember that after winding the first field wire in one direction, you must wind the other set of field windings in the opposite direction. When you unwind the field, be sure to note the direction of each field winding.

Figure VIII-1   Operating Box Car With Body Removed

Figure VIII-1 shows an operating box car with the body removed. It was removed by pulling the four pins on the underside of the chassis.

Figure VIII-2 shows how to restore a weak spring by collapsing it completely and then pulling each coil out one at a time and stretching the coil as you pull it. In this way, you do not have to take the solenoid apart to fix the spring, which should now move the plunger and close the box car door. To help this closing motion, apply TV contact cleaner on the moving parts of the mechanism to remove any dirt and then add a light lubrication that does not pick up dust.

Solenoids can burn out if overworked, although your circuit breaker should prevent this from happening by tripping first. If you must replace a solenoid, remember that it is a coil of wire which is fairly easy to rewind. Use enameled wire, similar to that used in rewinding fields and armatures. Since the solenoid is a simple coil, it is easier to wind than the more complex armatures or fields. First count the turns on the original solenoid coil, then remove all the old wire and turn the solenoid core while you feed the wire in an even back-and-forth motion. If you have a speed control on your electric drill, you can speed up the process by having the drill do the turning. Figure VIII-3 shows how. After you have rewound the coil of wire, fix the windings with a small amount of glue such as Duco Cement.

Other motor-driven accessories, such as the saw mill, oil drum loader, log loader, etc., use an induction motor. I have never encountered an inoperative induction motor and doubt that they would break down under normal use. To be sure that this does not happen, ascertain that the drive train in these accessories is free from dirt and that any mechanical binding that could stall the motor is cleaned away. Sometimes a lever in one of these complex accessories will over-run its throw and cause the whole motor to stop.

Fixing such a problem requires us to look at the sequence of motions, sometimes running the accessory backwards to unbind the problem. Most of all be patient and never force the issue. If you cannot get the bug out immediately wait a while before trying again. A fresh start on a problem works wonders!

If an induction motor does burn out, it will, unfortunately, have to be replaced, since the home workshop is not equipped to rewind their stator or field. A special jig is used for this purpose.

The "Talking Station" was invented by one of Gilbert's most prolific contributors. "Smitty" came up with the idea of a station that would have a recorded announcement, stop the train and restart it on cue. For 1940, this was quite a tall order since it also had to withstand the hands of children! The engineering was excellent, but the name, "A-Koostikin,"

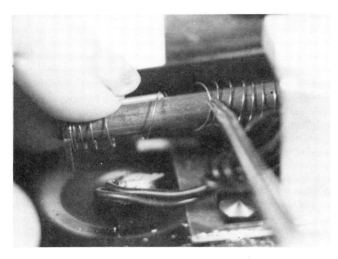

Figure VIII-2   Stretching A Spring

was a bit much for the customers. When the same device was renamed "The Talking Station," it became a big seller. If you have one, you will find it an ingenious combination of cams and gears. The record for the station is still available in small quantities at train meets or from a few dealers. You should write to the larger dealers, who may advertise in the **S Gaugian** magazine, and inquire if they have the record. It could cost from $10 to $20.

The first thing I did when I got my station working was to make a tape recording of the record. The record is a 78 RPM, 4.75 inch miniature that has two sides so that if one side is scratchy you can try the other.

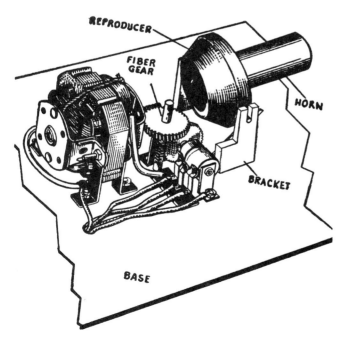

Figure VIII-4   Talking Station Cam and Contact Arm

The station's instructions even show you how to change the record. The record is timed to the cam shown in the circled part of Figure VIII-4. Should the train fail to start on cue, check the contact finger at the arrow. It should be in contact

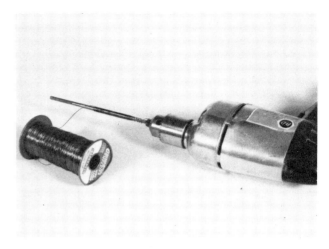

Figure VIII-3   Winding A Solenoid On A Drill

with the cam when the mechanism is not operating or is in the "off" position. If the contact arm is not touching the cam, bend it down so that it just touches. Do not bend it so far that it reaches the cut-out part of the cam or the engine and train will not stop at the proper time. This should be the only adjustment necessary for this accessory and it will really enhance your pike.

Another attention-getter is the cattle loader—a personal contribution of A. C. Gilbert himself. It works on the idea of vibrating a special rough paper on which the cows' feet move. The accessory's downfall however is that the original cow's feet material was wool and when invaded by moths was devoured so that most of the cows from the 1950s lack feet. I searched for many years to find a substitute for the directional cloth material and finally found it in the paint department of a hardware store. The material is sold under the name of "Shur-Line" paint pads. It is a white, directional nap material mounted on a plastic base. You can buy refill pads and cut them with heavy shears to fit the cows' feet.

For proper operation it is important to mount the one-way cloth correctly on the cow bases. The fiber direction should not be straight back, but at a slight, 15 to 30 degree angle to the base. This gives a forward and side motion to keep the cows moving around the perimeter of the corral. Since the black cows belong in the lefthand corral and the brown ones in the right, the angle slant for the black cows is opposite that of the brown cows. Figure VIII-5 shows the proper angles from underneath.

To "re-foot" a moth-eaten cow's foot, remove the damaged material with a knife. Be sure that the plastic surface is smooth and without any residual cloth hanging on. Cut a one-and-a-quarter inch piece of new material and round its edges. Glue it to the cow, as shown in Figure VIII-5, and trim off any excess material. In applying the cloth be sure that the tips of the fiber go toward the tail or the cow will move backwards!

The Animated Station uses the same concept to move its people around. When these people need new shoes treat them as you did the brown cows and cut out new shoes from the Shur-Line pad as depicted in Figure VIII-5.

Accessories are fun to add to your pike. The following pages of information and how-to instructions from the Gilbert Instruction Sheets will help you to hook up and operate your accessories.

Viewed From The Bottom

Black cow goes
in left corral

Brown cow goes
in right corral

Figure VIII-5 Direction For Cow's Feet Material

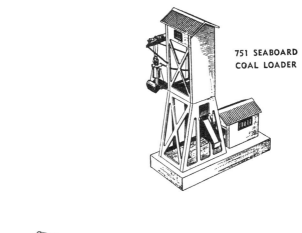

758 "SAM" THE SEMAPHORE MAN

751 SEABOARD
COAL LOADER

QUIETING THE BRAKEMAN

A solenoid, a simple electrical device, is an essential feature of accessory operation. Most A. F. accessories depending on a solenoid for action operate on 60 cycle AC current which creates a constant chattering noise. The noise is distracting and usually unwanted. One particular accessory that chatters incessantly is the #977 brakeman caboose. In the brakeman's case the solenoid pulls the brakeman in while the train is running. While the brakeman is being moved there is a loud buzzing that mars the realism of our railroad's operations.

There is a very simple solution to this problem. As shown in the wiring diagram in Figure VIII-6 if you place a DC rectifier between the solenoid and the power pick-up on the caboose the brakeman will work quietly. You will have to open up the car to get into the caboose's interior. This requires careful and patient twisting and a bit of bending of the brakeman's connecting rod to the solenoid. You will need to work slowly in order not to break anything. A 1-amp full wave rectifier bridge (such as found at Radio Shack, #726-1161) will do the job well. Be sure to insulate the connections with electrical tape after you have soldered the wires together.

752 LOG LOADER

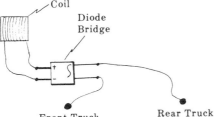
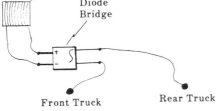

Coil

Diode
Bridge

Front Truck

Rear Truck

Figure VIII-6 Quieting the Buzz of the #977 Brakeman Caboose

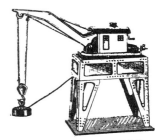

583 ELECTROMATIC CRANE

APPENDIX

HOOK UP AND OPERATION OF AUTOMATIC ACTION CARS

The current to operate the cars is picked up by two metal wheels on one car truck which should run on the rail which has the BASE POST side of the current, and by finger type pickup which protrudes from one of the truck sides and makes contact with the special rail section supplied with the car. This section is connected to the 15 volt side of the current and only energized when the control box button is pressed.

ATTACHING THE SPECIAL PICKUP SECTION

There are two types of pickup sections used: one is a snap-on type and the other, a clamp-on type. The snap-on type fastens to the track as shown in Figure VIII-6.

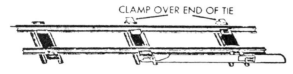

FIGURE VIII-6
SNAP-ON PICK UP SECTION

It is used to operate cars such as the Automobile Unloading Car, Log Dump Car, Coal Dump Car, and Operating Box Car.

The clamp-on type is shown in Figure VIII-7. For best operation there should be straight track on both sides of the pickup section.

Nest bottom of the rail under metal part B. Then close locking lever A on the other rail, as shown above.

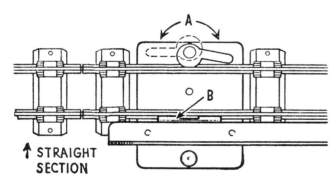

FIGURE VIII-7 -8
CLAMP-ON PICK UP SECTION

HOW TO HOOK UP AND OPERATE THE NO. 718 MAIL PICK-UP CAR

First determine a straight section in your layout where you wish to pick up and unload the mail bags.

Then attach the No. 713 Special Rail Section as follows:

With the Locking Lever A facing left as shown by the dotted line in Figure VIII-8, insert the fiber base of the special rail section between the first and second ties on the desired section of straight track. See that the bottom portion of the outside rail rests underneath the raised part of the metal strip B, then turn the Locking Lever A to the right as far as it will go, so it clamps over the bottom of the inside rail. As shown in Figure VIII-8 there must be at least one section of straight track in front of the special rail section so that any rolling stock coming out of a curve will not overhang enough to cause interference.

The car should be placed on the track so the small metal contact shoe which protrudes from one of the tracks, is on the same side as the special contact rail on the No. 713.

WIRING TO A TRANSFORMER

Connect the transformer to the track terminal. Connect the **LONG YELLOW** wire from the terminal post on the No. 713 Special Rail Section to a clip underneath the control box. Connect the **SHORT YELLOW** wire from the other control box clip to the **15 VOLT POST** on the transformer.

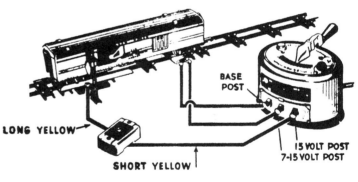

FIGURE VIII-9
718 WIRING

DIRECTIONS FOR WIRING TO A NO. 14 RECTIFORMER

Follow the above instructions, only hook the **SHORT YELLOW** wire to the Alternating Current post nearest the center of the Rectiformer.

Place the car on the track so that the opening and hook on the car are toward the front of the train, on the same side of the track as the special contact rail No. 713, and the train should be run in a forward direction. See Figure VIII-9.

Hang one of the mail bags on the standard, start the train and as it approaches the special track section, press the button and hold it down. When the mail car passes over the special track, the hook will swing out and pick up the mail bag.

After the car has passed, release the button. Hang the other mail bag on the standard and repeat the operation just mentioned, and the car will automatically pick up the mail bag and deliver the one it picked up on the first trip.

MECHANICAL CARS:

No. 25071 Tie Jector (American Flyer), No. 25081 Hay Jector (NYC) and No. 25082 Hay Jector (New Haven) Cars

This car is designed to be used on both Gilbert Pike Master track and Standard S Gauge Track. If packed with an American Flyer Train Set, the activating trip designed for Pike Master track was included. If you purchased this car separately, you will find two activating trips—one to fit Pike Master track, and one to fit Standard S track. Select the trip which fits the type of track you have in your layout.

ATTACHING THE TRIP TO THE TRACK

The trip for use on the Pike Master track is snapped into position as shown below in Figure VIII-10.

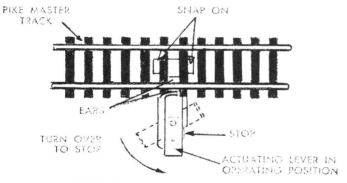

FIGURE VIII-10
SNAP-ON TRIP FOR PIKE MASTER TRACK

The trip for use on standard American Flyer track is fastened into position by slipping the edge of one rail under the rail retainer and lock the cam against the other rail, as shown below. These trips are designed for use on straight track sections only.

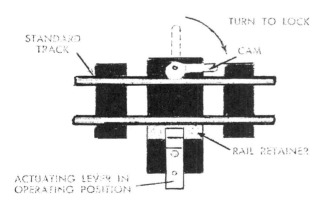

FIGURE VIII-11
TRIP FOR AMERICAN FLYER TRACK

OPERATING THE CAR

Place the Action Car on the track so that the operating arm is on the same side of the track as the actuating lever on the trip. Place the bales or ties into the top of the chute on the car. When the activating lever on the trip is in operating position and the car passes it in the direction indicated in Figures VIII-12 or VIII-13, a bale or tie will be automatically ejected.

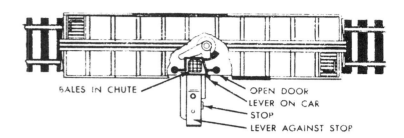

FIGURE VIII-12
HAY JECTOR

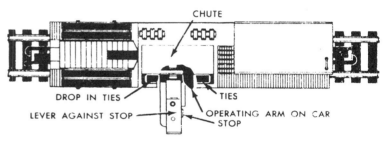

FIGURE VIII-13
TIE JECTOR

Do not close the Hay Jector door after placing bales in the car. If you do not want the car to operate, swing the actuating lever on the trip out of the operating position.

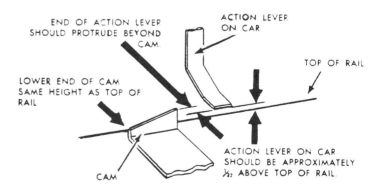

Each action lever and the cam portion of the track trips are factory adjusted. If these adjustments should change, they can be corrected by bending slightly as shown in the diagram above. Then make sure that the car's action lever does not bind after adjusting it.

41

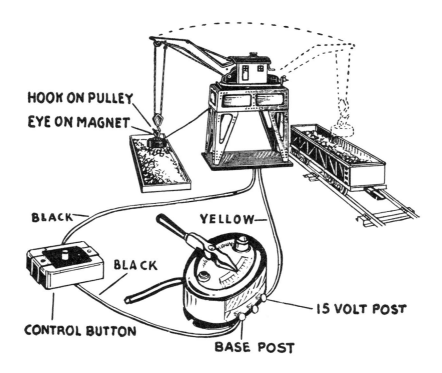

HOOK ON PULLEY
EYE ON MAGNET
BLACK
BLACK
YELLOW
15 VOLT POST
CONTROL BUTTON
BASE POST

FIGURE VIII-14
CRANE HOOK UP

CONNECTING AND OPERATING
No. 583 ELECTROMATIC CRANE

Place Crane in position in your layout. The illustration below shows the best arrangement of the Crane in relation to track. Hook it up as follows:

Connect the YELLOW wire from the Crane to the **15 VOLT POST** of the transformer. Then connect the BLACK wire from the Crane to one of the clips underneath the Control Button. Lastly connect the short BLACK wire from the other Control Box clip to the **BASE POST** on the transformer. The illustration shows the standard method of wiring the transformer to a track layout.

The Crane is equipped with a sequence reversing switch which performs a cycle of four steps—Right—Neutral—Left —Neutral. Push the button, if the Crane does not move, release and push again. The Crane will now move in one direction until pressure on the button is released. To make Crane move in the opposite direction, push the button twice and hold down. In operating, do not allow Crane to move more than one-half revolution.

After you operate the Crane once you can place it the proper distance from the rail to obtain the best position for picking the load up from the tray and dropping it into the car.

The hand wheel at the rear of the cab raises and lowers the boom so you can place the magnet at the proper height over the scrap iron load.

CONNECTING AND OPERATING THE
No. 583-A ELECTROMATIC CRANE

Connect YELLOW wire from control box to **15 VOLT POST** on transformer, then connect BLACK wire from the control box to the base post on the transformer.

When using a transformer and a No. 15 rectiformer, connect the wires from the control box directly to the transformer as described in the above paragraphs.

When using a No. 14 or 16 Electronic Rectiformer connect the BLACK and YELLOW wires from the control box to the two **ALTERNATING CURRENT POSTS** on the rectiformers.

The Crane is equipped with a two button control box and a double wound motor.

Pushing the red button will cause the cab and boom to rotate in one direction, pushing the green button causes the motor to run in the opposite direction. Pushing either button will cause the electro magnet to be energized to pick up steel scrap. When the button is released the motor will stop and steel scrap will be released.

In operating do not allow the Crane to revolve more than one-half revolution.

After you operate the Crane once you can place it the proper distance from the rail to obtain the best position for picking the load up from the tray and dropping it into the car.

The hand wheel at the rear of the cab raises and lowers the boom so that you can adjust the magnet at the proper heights over the scrap iron load.

The illustration below shows the best arrangement for the Crane in relation to track. Hook it up as follows:

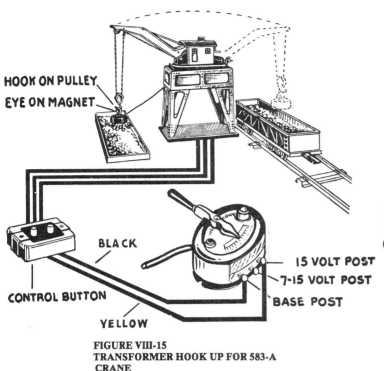

FIGURE VIII-15
TRANSFORMER HOOK UP FOR 583-A
CRANE

LOADING LOGS: THE No. 751 LOG LOADER

Place the log loader in front of a section of straight track. Connect the BLACK wire of the RAINBOW CABLE to the BASE POST on the transformer. Then connect the YELLOW wire from the control box to the **15 VOLT POST** on the transformer.

If you are using a No. 14 Electronic Rectiformer, hook the BLACK and YELLOW wires to the two **ALTERNATING CURRENT** posts. Place the three logs on the Log Loader platform and the Log Loader is ready to operate.

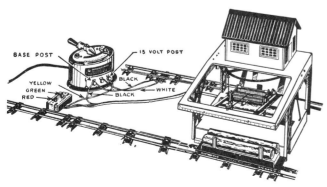

FIGURE VIII-16
LOG LOADER

Press the **GREEN** button on the control box and one of the logs will be elevated to the carriage. Press the **RED** button on the control box and the carriage will convey the log to the end of the arms and deposit it automatically into the empty car below, then return for a repeat operation.

Due to atmospheric conditions or use, the string which is used to elevate the carriage may stretch and become too long, thereby not allowing the log to release. If this happens, turn the nickel plated adjusting nut on the end of the carriage release rod or shorten the string a little.

If you have a No. 717 Automatic Log Dump Car you can run a spur track to the back of the Log Loader, dump the logs automatically, then bring the train around to the front and have it loaded again.

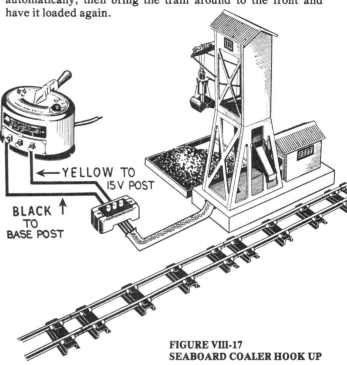

FIGURE VIII-17
SEABOARD COALER HOOK UP

Setting Up and Operating the No. 752 Seaboard Coaler

Check to see that the ends of the formed wire brace are in the holes in the upright sides and that the cord is running through the various pulleys. Then place the Coal Loader in the desired position in your track layout so that the chute is over the track and the coal will fall into the car below.

If you are using a transformer, connect the **BLACK** wire to the **BASE POST** on the transformer. Then, connect the **YELLOW** wire to the **15 VOLT POST.**

If you are using a No. 14 Rectiformer, connect the **YELLOW** and **BLACK** wires to the two **ALTERNATING CURRENT TAPS.** Now press the **GREEN** button, on the Control Box, and the bucket will be lowered to the coal pile. Press the **RED** button partially down and the jaws will clamp together. Press it all the way down, and the bucket will be elevated to the tower. Release the button and the coal will fall down the chute to the car.

Oiling: Bearings and gears on the motor located in the engine house can be oiled by removing the roof and through the door. A few drops of light oil is all that is necessary.

SETTING UP AND OPERATING
NO. 755 TALKING STATION

The Talking Station is designed to operate on 60 cycle current only. It will operate from a transformer running the train on ALTERNATING CURRENT or from a transformer and rectifer running the train on DIRECT CURRENT.

First determine the approximate position in your layout where you want the station located, then remove the steel pin from the outside rail and replace it with a fiber track pin, then several sections away repeat this operation to give you two or three sections of rail which are completely insulated from the rest of the track.

Next clip the No. 707 Track Terminal on the track so the BASE POST CLIP is connected to the insulated rail.

If you are using a TRANSFORMER only to operate the train on ALTERNATING CURRENT follow the wiring diagram in Figure VIII-18 below.

If you are using a TRANSFORMER and a No. 15 DIRECT-RONIC RECTIFIER to operate the train on DIRECT CUR-RENT follow the wiring diagram in Figure VIII-19.

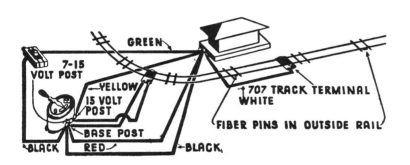

FIGURE VIII-18
TALKING STATION WIRED FOR AC

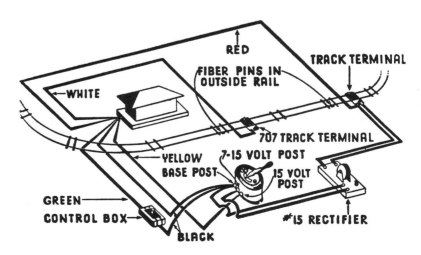

FIGURE VIII-19
TRANSFORMER AND DIRECTRONIC RECTIFIER
FOR DC OPERATION

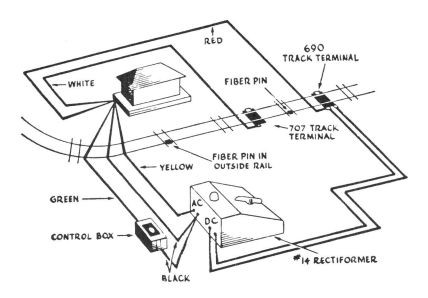

FIGURE VIII-20
ELECTRONIC RECTIFORMER FOR DC OPERATIONS

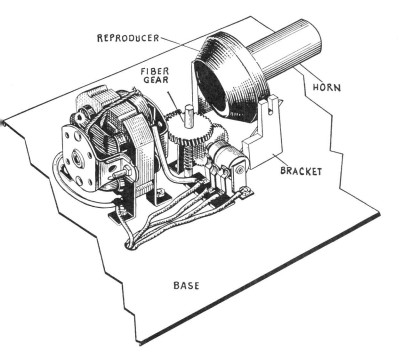

If you are using a No. 14 Electronic Rectiformer to operate the train on Direct Current, follow the wiring diagram in Figure VIII-20.

Next remove the cork from the needle in the reproducer and attach the horn to the reproducer neck—then insert the reproducer into the unit (as shown below) so the horn faces away from the motor and the two pins fit into the slots on the upright brackets and the needle is resting on the record.

Now start the train, and as it approaches the station and the insulated portion of the track, press the control box button, and the train will stop at the station while the train announcer makes his announcement. Then with a series of train noises the train will automatically start and run until you again press the button for a repeat performance. NOTE: on a small oval of track do not press the button a second time until the train has made several revolutions and the motor in the station has come to a stop.

Oiling

Keep all bearings well oiled, lubricate the gears with a small amount of vaseline or thin grease. If the lamps should burn out, replace with either a 14 or 18 volt lamp. For maximum sound open the station doors.

To Change the Record

To change the record remove the nut at the end of the turn-table shaft, as shown in Figure VIII-21. Slide the turntable and the record off the shaft, turn the record over and replace on the shaft with the turntable and washer. Tighten up on the nut. Replace the needle with any chrome plated needle every fifty times.

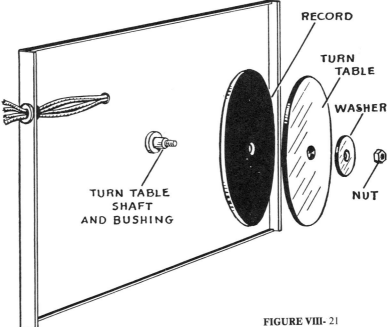

FIGURE VIII- 21

**SETTING UP AND OPERATING
"SAM" THE SEMAPHORE MAN (NO. 758-A)**

Remove a steel pin from the outside rail in front of the place you want the Semaphore stationed, and replace with a fiber pin; several sections of track from this fiber pin repeat this operation. This will give you two or three sections of rail which are completely insulated from the rest of the track.

Fasten the **No. 707 TRACK TERMINAL** on the track so the

BASE POST CLIP is connected to the outside rail in this insulated section. Connect one end of the separate **WHITE** wire which comes with the unit to the clip on the **No. 707 TRACK TERMINAL.** Connect the other end of the **WHITE** wire to the clip on the back edge of the semaphore base.

If you are using a transformer and Alternating Current see Figure VIII-22.

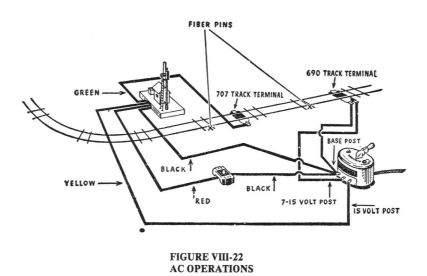

FIGURE VIII-22
AC OPERATIONS

46

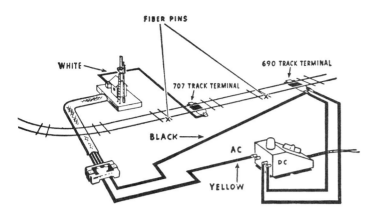

FIBER PINS

WHITE

690 TRACK TERMINAL

707 TRACK TERMINAL

BLACK

AC

DC

YELLOW

FIGURE VIII-23
RECTIFORMER FOR DIRECT CURRENT OPERATION

Connect the **BLACK** wire from the Control Box to the **BASE POST** on the transformer. Then, connect the **YELLOW** wire from the Control Box to the **15 VOLT POST** on the transformer. If you are using a No. 14 Electronic Rectiformer see Figure VIII-23.

Connect the **BLACK** wire from the Control Box to the **BASE POST** on the **No. 690 TRACK TERMINAL** which supplies current to the track. Then, connect the **YELLOW** wire from the Control Box to the **OUTSIDE A.C. POST** on the Rectiformer.

OPERATING THE NO. 766
ANIMATED STATION PLATFORM AND CAR

The No. 766 Animated Station Platform and Car unit consists of the following: 1—No. 766 Animated Station Platform, 1—No. 735 Operating Coach, 1—Control Box Unit, 2—Wood Screws for Mounting the Control Box and 4—Miniature People

To install this unit, place it in a portion of the layout so there are at least two straight tracks to mount on the platform base. Nest the straight track between the tie holders as shown in Figure VIII-24.
If only two sections of straight track are used, the station is to be placed on the inside of the oval. If more than two sections of straight track are used, the station can be placed on either side of the track.

Now open the gate fence and the one car door in front of it. As the people approach the car, press the red button on the Control Box which energizes the mat in the car and the people will walk from the platform into the car. Be sure the door at

opposite end of the car is closed or people will continue through the car and back onto the platform. Run the train around the track and stop it so the car is again in position. Open the door at the opposite end of the car, press the red button and people will walk out of the car onto the platform.

Connect **BLACK WIRE** from the platform to the transformer's **BASE POST**. Next connect the **RED WIRE** from the platform to the wire clip under the red button on the Control Box. Connect the **YELLOW WIRE** from the platform to the remaining spring clip on the Control Box. Finally, connect the **YELLOW WIRE** from the Control Box to the **15 VOLT POST** on the transformer.

If this unit is used on a layout powered with a transformer do not use the **TWO BLACK WIRES** on the control box. They can be clipped off and discarded.

If the unit is used on a layout run by direct current and powered by a transformer and rectifier, connect one **BLACK**

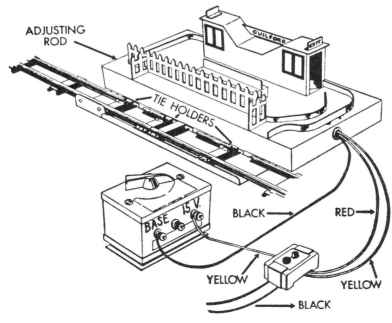

ADJUSTING ROD

TIE HOLDERS

BASE 15 V.

BLACK   RED

YELLOW   YELLOW

BLACK

FIGURE VIII-24
TRANSFORMER HOOK UP

WIRE to the BASE POST on the transformer and the other BLACK WIRE to the BASE POST clip on the track terminal.

If the unit is used on a layout powered by a No. 16 Rectiformer connect one BLACK WIRE to the inside A C POST and the other BLACK WIRE to the BASE POST clip on the track terminal.

To operate: place the people on the platform near the swinging gate, with the gate closed, then turn on the rotary switch on the Control Box. This will cause the floor mat to vibrate and the people will "walk" around the platform, down one ramp and up the other and continue to walk around.

The car should be placed on the track so the side with two movable doors faces the platform, and the metal wheels on the one truck ride on the rail which has the Base Post current. If your layout is wired so the Base Post current is in the other

rail than that which the metal wheels are on, spread the truck slightly, remove the wheel and axle assemblies and reverse the position of the wheels.

Due to variations in the line voltage it may be necessary to adjust for the correct amount of vibration. To adjust: turn the adjusting rod, located on the opposite side of the platform from the wires. If the unit vibrates too fast or too slow, turn the adjusting lever rod slowly. Start by turning in a clockwise direction for several revolutions; if the unit does not respond, turn the rod in a counter-clockwise direction.

Run the train around the track and stop it so the operating coach is positioned in front of the platform. See that the outside of the movable doors are located at the edge of the floor mat. When the car is in this position the contact finger from the car truck should be resting on the contact strip which is attached to the platform.

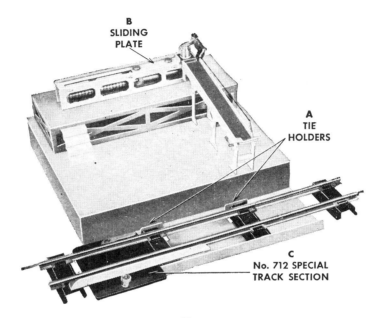

FIGURE VIII-25
No. 770 LOADING PLATFORM

OPERATING THE NO. 770 LOADING PLATFORM

To install, place it in the layout so it is along a straight portion of the track. Then nest the track between the tie holders, "A" as shown.

To hook up to a transformer, and a No. 15 Rectifier, connect the YELLOW wire to the 15 VOLT POST on the transformer. Then connect the BLACK wire from the platform to one of the clips underneath the control box. Connect the SHORT BLACK wire from the other control box clip to the BASE POST on the transformer.

For a No. 14 or 16 Rectiformer, connect the YELLOW wire to one of the ALTERNATING CURRENT Posts on the Rectiformer. Connect the BLACK wire from the platform to one of the clips underneath the Control Box. Then, connect the SHORT BLACK wire from the other Control Box Clip to the other ALTERNATING CURRENT Post on the Rectiformer.

Push the button on the Control Box -- the man on the platform will go forward; when the button is released the man will return to his original position and be waiting for work.

Next pull back the sliding Plate B in Figure VIII-25 and place the four boxes or milk cans on the runway. They will be fed automatically to the man by spring pressure. Each time the button is pushed he will shove one of the units down the chute and onto or into a car which is waiting to receive the merchandise—when the man goes back to his original position he raises the chute end so it will not interfer with any passing rolling stock.

When using the Loading Platform with the No. 732 or No. 734 Operating Cars be sure that the No. 712 Special Track Section is positioned on the track as shown at C.

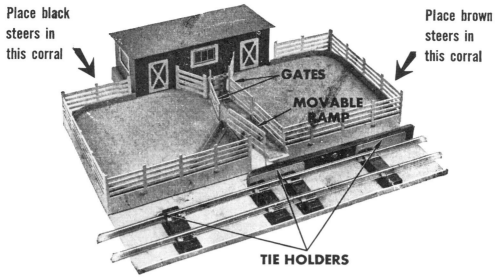

Place black steers in this corral

Place brown steers in this corral

GATES

MOVABLE RAMP

TIE HOLDERS

THE NO. 771 STOCK YARD AND CAR

The No. 771 Operating Stock Yard and Car Unit consists of: 1—No. 771 Stock Yard, 1—No. 736 Stock Car, 1—Control Box Unit, 2—Wood screws for mounting the control box and, 8–Miniature steers.

To install, place it in a portion of the layout so there are at least two straight tracks to mount on the stock yard base—nest the straight track between the tie holders as shown in Figure VIII-26.

Connect **BLACK WIRE** from Stock Yard to **BASE POST** on transformer. Connect **RED WIRE** from Stock Yard to wire clip under the red button on Control Box. Then connect **YELLOW WIRE** from Stock Yard to remaining spring clip on Control Box and connect **YELLOW WIRE** from Control Box to **15 VOLT POST** on Transformer.

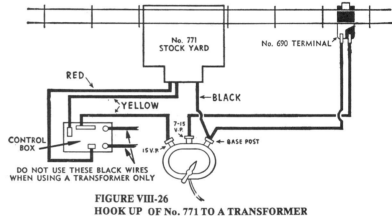

No. 771 STOCK YARD

No. 690 TERMINAL

RED

YELLOW

BLACK

CONTROL BOX

7-15 V.P.

15 V.P.

BASE POST

DO NOT USE THESE BLACK WIRES WHEN USING A TRANSFORMER ONLY

FIGURE VIII-26
HOOK UP OF No. 771 TO A TRANSFORMER

OPERATING THE NO. 779 OIL DRUM LOADER

Place the oil drum loader along a section of straight track as shown in the drawing below. After it operates, the loader may have to be moved a little so that the drums dump into the Gondola Car. When a correct location is found, the unit can be fastened down by inserting screws through the holes located on the lower step and the end of the platform, as shown below.

Connect the yellow wire from one of the terminals on the oil drum loader to the 15 volt post on the transformer. Connect the long black wire from the other terminal on the oil drum loader to one of the clips underneath the Control Box. Then, connect the short black wire from the other Control Box clip to the base post on the transformer. The unit is now ready to operate. Turn the Control Box switch one-half turn clockwise. The motor should run and cause the operating arm to move back and forth at about a 90° movement. Next stop the motor by turning off the switch, place the truck and truckman on the operating arm so the end pin locates in the hole on the underneath side of the truck. Place the oil drums in the chute so they roll down to the unloading platform. Now turn the switch back on and the truckman should pick up one drum at a time, bring it to the car (a regular Gondola Car is recommended) and dump it.

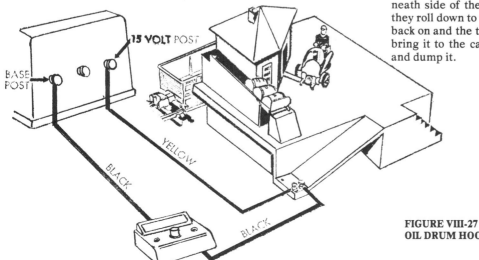

15 VOLT POST

BASE POST

YELLOW

BLACK

BLACK

FIGURE VIII-27
OIL DRUM HOOK UP

USING THE
NO. 787 LOG LOADER

Check to see that the small piece of tape which holds the carriage and hook to the front of the elevated track is in place. Place loader either along a mainline or between two lines of track as the logs can be dumped onto either side of the platform if you are using a Log Dump Car.

Next, fasten the YELLOW wire from one of the TERMINAL POSTS on the log loader to the **15 or 18 VOLT POST** on the transformer. Connect the long BLACK wire from the other TERMINAL on the loader to one of the CLIPS underneath the control box. Connect the short BLACK wire from the other control box clip to the BASE POST on the transformer. Place or dump the logs on the platform of the loader.

Now press the control box button and hold it down. The carriage will descend and the hook will pick up one log which has been raised for it. The log will then be transported up over the car and dropped so it lands onto the car below. Any Gondola or Flat Car with stakes can be used but much more play value will result if a Log Dump Car is used.

The gears and rotor shaft can be lubricated by removing the roof. Use a light grease or vaseline on the gears and a light oil on the shafts and bearings.

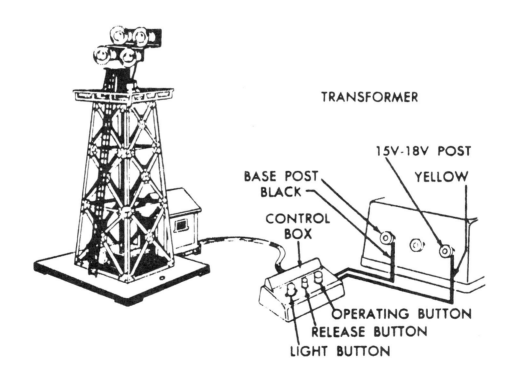

ASSEMBLING AND OPERATING THE
NO. 23780 GABE, THE LAMPLIGHTER

To assemble, place the roof on the house. Check to see that the string is free and that the man moves up and down the ladder freely.

Attach the black lead wire from the control box to the base post of the transformer and the yellow lead wire to the 15-18 volt post, as shown in Figure VIII-27.

To operate, press down, and then release, the green button (right side of control box). This will cause the man to climb up the ladder. Repeat this operation until the man reaches the top of the ladder. Press down the red button (left side of control box) and turn approximately one-quarter of a turn to light lamps. To return man to base of ladder press down center button on control box. To turn off lights, turn red button back to original position so it will raise up and break contact.

OPERATING THE NO. 785 COAL LOADER

First, check to see that the track brace is inserted into the slots at the lower end of the track. Then, position the Loader in the desired location on your layout so that the track (either the main or spur line) runs through the center of the Loader uprights. Place the storage bin alongside the Loader and fill with coal, ballast or fine gravel.

Then, attach the BLACK wire from the control box to the base post terminal on the transformer. Attach the YELLOW wire to the 15 or 18 volt transformer post.

The Loader is now ready to operate. Press the Green Button and the Grab Bucket will come down to the coal pile with its jaws open. Press the Red Button part-way down and the jaws

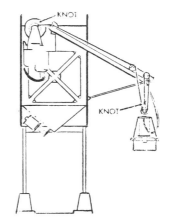

will snap shut, gathering up a quantity of coal or stone. Press the Red Button all the way down and the bucket will rise and ride up into the tower. Release the Red Button and the load will drop into the coal hopper.

Run the train around the track and stop either a Gondola, Hopper or Coal Dump Car under the Coal Hopper. Press the center button and the material will fall into the car below.

Bearings and gears on the motor, located in the tower, can be oiled by removing the roof and through the side openings. A few drops of light machine-type oil is all that is necessary.

If the string which raises and lowers the bucket should tear or break, you can replace it.

Use a piece of good, strong flexible string 3-1/2 feet long (light braided fish line is fine). Tie a large enough knot in one end of the string so that it will not pull through the hole in the spool flange. Insert the unknotted end through the hole in the spool flange from the outside and pull the string through the knot. Run the string over the axle rod at the top of the track, then down over pulley No. 1 on the track, down and around pulley No. 2 on the bucket, up and around pulley No. 3 on the truck, then back down to the bucket and tie the end to the bucket handle.

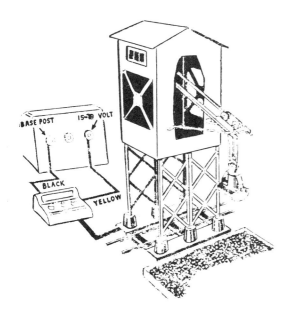

THE NO. 23791
COW ON THE TRACK

To hook up and operate the cow, study Figure VIII-28 and proceed as follows:

First, determine the item's location in the layout, keeping in mind that while the cow is on the track, the train will be stopped and when the cow leaves the track the train will proceed. Then remove two metal track pins from the rails and replace them with the two fiber insulating pins. These pins should be about three track sections apart. Now connect the No. 707 Track Terminal to this insulated portion of the track.

Connect the WHITE WIRE from the No. 1 POST to the 707 TRACK TERMINAL. Connect the GREEN WIRE from the control box to POST No. 2. Connect the RED WIRE from the control box to POST No. 4, the YELLOW WIRE to the **15 or 18 VOLT POST** and the BLACK WIRE between POST No. 3 on the accessory and the BASE POST on the transformer.

The unit is now ready to operate. When the red button on the control box is pushed the cow will walk onto the track. This will kill the track voltage in the insulated section and stop the train. When the green button is pressed the cow will leave the track and the train will proceed.

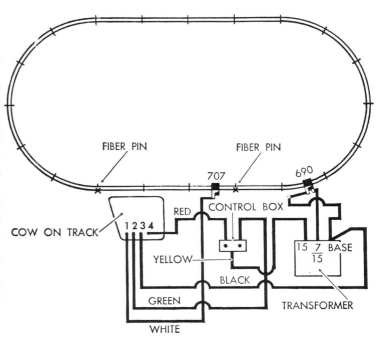

FIGURE VIII-28   LAMPLIGHTER WIRING

ASSEMBLING AND
OPERATING THE NO. 23796 SAW MILL

If not assembled, remove saw mill from box and assemble boom and cab to house, passing end of boom through cutout in front of house and hooking end of boom into slot in rear of house. Check to see that string is free and in pulleys, and that hook swings freely in cab. (Remove piece of tape holding hook to cab during shipment.)

Position man in cab inserting (2) projections on feet of man into holes in cab as shown below. Use a little household cement to fasten man to cab if necessary. Place sawdust pile on base, matching locating pins on pile with holes in base. Place two roofs in position on building.

Place saw mill along section of main or spur straight track. After unit is in operation it may be necessary to move it a little so that lumber drops properly into the gondola car. Unit may be then fastened down permanently with two wood screws (inserting screws through holes at opposite corners of base).

WIRING

Connect the YELLOW wire from one of the TERMINAL POSTS on the saw mill to the **15 or 18 VOLT POST** on the transformer.

Connect the long BLACK wire from the other TERMINAL POST on the saw mill to one of the clips underneath the CONTROL BOX.

Connect the short BLACK wire from the other CONTROL BOX clip to the BASE POST on the transformer, as shown above.

OPERATION

Check operation of the saw mill before loading lumber. Press the control box button and hold it down. Cab should move freely up and down the boom and log car should travel back and forth across base.

Now insert pieces of lumber, ONE AT A TIME, into slot in side of house. Be sure to load each piece of lumber HORIZONTALLY, not vertically, as board may jam during operation if it is not lying flat.

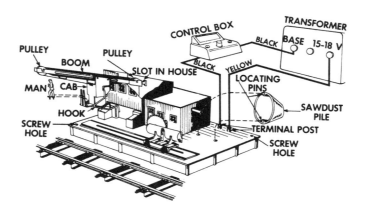

Chapter IX
OPERATING WITH 2-RAIL TRACK

When Gilbert decided in the early 1940s to make the move to two-rail track for a new line of realistic model trains, some important engineering modifications to track plans and operations had to be considered.

Probably at the top of the list of specialized 2-rail track plans was the reverse loop. This popular layout feature allows a train to turn around on itself. Unfortunately, with a 2-rail system, the electricity does the same thing and will short-out the power supply because rail 1, at first on the outside, turns around in the reverse loop and becomes rail 2. The effect on the electrical system is the same as connecting the base post directly to the 7-15 volt post — a direct short across the terminals. See Figure IX-1 below.

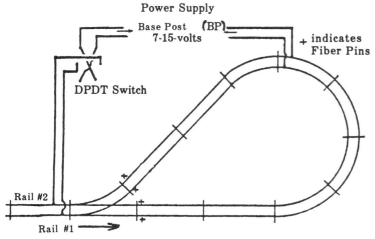

Figure IX-1 Isolating the Reverse Loop

The Gilbert systems to overcome the reverse loop shorting problems were a bit complicated, so here is a simpler solution. You will need a double pole, double throw switch, four fiber pins and sufficient wire. When you operate the loop, you will also have to be on the alert to avoid unintentionally stopping the train.

The wiring concept is to isolate the train while you change the polarity of the switched track. This is easily accomplished by isolating the entire loop from the track switch with fiber pins (or air gaps if you have your tracks nailed down).

If you have difficulty obtaining fiber pins, remember that besides having an insulating material connecting the rails, you should have a separator keeping the tracks from touching. The gap should be 1/16" (no larger) to allow the pickup wheels to cross the insulating section without interrupting the current flow. The fiber pin is a T-shaped connector which accomplishes this objective.

Figure IX-1, shows how to place the fiber pins to isolate the loop as well as proper connection to the power source. Notice, too, that the loop is powered with a separate set of wires and is isolated on both rails. As the engine travels in the direction of the arrow along the straight section of the switch, the polarity of the current is set so that the loop is the same as the straight section. If the double pole, double throw (DPDT) switch is improperly set, the train will reach the fiber pin connection, spark and stall. If left there, the circuit breaker will eventually trip as you short the circuit through the motor. For a second or two this is not harmful and is an easy way to test the position of the DPDT switch.

The wiring of the DPDT switch is quite easy. If you have wired a switch for direct current polarity reversing, it is the same method. Figure IX-2 shows the underside of a DPDT. The center lugs on the switch go to the track, and the outside ones just crisscross to change the polarity.

Operation is simple. Mount the DPDT so that it is adjacent to the switch control box. When you throw the switch you will also reverse the polarity by using the DPDT. Of course, you will want the loop part of the layout to be large enough to accommodate your longest train. As this wiring diagram is set up, you may throw the switches after the last car has passed through the switch. If you have one reverse loop you will probably need to put another one somewhere else in your pike to re-reverse the train. The wiring is exactly the same and, if you put two loops back-to-back, you need only one DPDT switch on the connecting line between the two loops.

To keep the DPDT set correctly, color-code the DPDT to correspond with the color of the light (red or green) of the switch box. So, if the light is green, the DPDT should be set toward the green mark.

This is fine for small layouts, but for a large pike with multi-train operation, I have found it better to have as many AUTOMATIC devices as possible to avoid rear-end collisions and other mishaps. The ideal method of switching the polarity for the reverse loop would have the switching action of the turnout do the job for you. This would mean that with the switching of the track direction, the polarity is reversed.

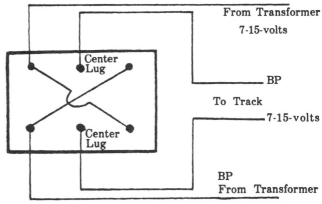

Figure IX-2 Double Pole, Double Throw Switch, Underside

SENSOR REQUIRED

The key to making the operation simple and automatic requires a slight modification to the American Flyer turnout. The parts are available at Radio Shack and can be installed in less than half-an-hour. To install the sensor, which is a subminiature roller/lever micro-switch, remove the bottom plates from the AF turnout. Locate the switching mechanism at the bottom of the turnout and note how the micro-switch fits as shown in Figure IX-3. Mark the position of the three leads from the micro-switch and file grooves into the ridge on the bottom of the turnout to allow the leads from the micro-switch to fit loosely.

Next, with a file, or more easily with a moto-tool grinder, cut a depression into the lever arm that throws the frog. The depression should be 3/16 inch deep and 3/8 inch long with a taper to allow a smooth action. Figure IX-4 is a template to help locate the position and grind the correct depression.

Figure IX-3 Sensor Switch

When the grinding is completed, locate the micro-switch in position and check its operation. When the roller is in the depression, you should be able to move the lever arm and hear a click. If this is not the case, then the depression needs to be deeper. You will need a shim under the micro-switch which can be a piece of cardboard 1/8 inch thick, and 1/2 inch by 3/4 inch. Hold the micro-switch in position and work the frog back and forth. The roller lever should run smoothly over the lever arm from the turnout's switch mechanism.

Solder a wire to the common (c) connection and the normally open (no) connection on the micro-switch. Place a piece of insulating material over the connections and put the bottom plates back on the turnout. The small bottom plate will hold the micro-switch in position.

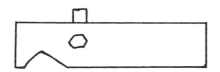

Figure IX-4 Grinding Template

WIRE TO RELAY

Now that the sensor is installed in the bottom of the turnout, you have a positive method of electrically sensing the position of the frog. Instead of having a double pole, double throw switch, you will use a DPDT relay. The sensor is used to activate the relay which is wired exactly like the DPDT switch. Now you have a method of building an automatic reverse loop with available materials in a short time. The materials, including the relay, will cost a little over $5. The relay should be a 12-volt DPDT design. Be sure to operate the relay on direct current, since AC will cause chatter and not give a good connection.

WIRING FOR AUTOMATIC REVERSE LOOPS

On the double pole, double throw relay there will be 8 contacts. Since each relay brand will probably differ, it is not possible to be more specific than the general diagram below. There are two connections (#7 and #8) that control the coil in the relay. These go to the 12-volt DC and the sense switch you installed in the turnout.

The contacts that are on the moving part of the relay go to the track. The stationary contacts on the relay are connected with the transformer as shown and cross under the relay.

Should there be a short with your initial connections when the train enters the loop, then simply reverse the connections on the portion of the diagram that is circled with a dashed line.

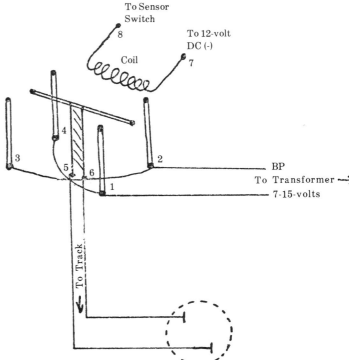

Figure IX-5 DPDT Relay   Connections #7 and #8 control the relay coil.

TURNOUTS GAPS AND BLOCKS

The manual or remote control turnouts supplied by Gilbert are equipped with a double pole, double throw switch which directs the flow of current to the track in the way the frog of the turnout is directing the train. The schematic diagram shows how this is done.

A single pole, single throw switch is also included to create a dead section when the frog is turned against an oncoming train. This can be used as a crude block signal to prevent accidents, but it was designed primarily to allow one train to be held on a siding while another passed by, as illustrated in Figure IX-6.

A more sophisticated system of blocks can be engineered with either the pressure type track trip or the electrical trip. The pressure type depends on the weight of the rolling stock and is a fairly finicky device. Besides that, it is necessary that the track NOT be fastened down in the area of this trip.

The electrical trip is a simple relay that only depends upon the current being drawn across it. When the engine passes over the controlling section, the track trip is energized and throws a switch to activate the accessory or turn on a controlled section of track.

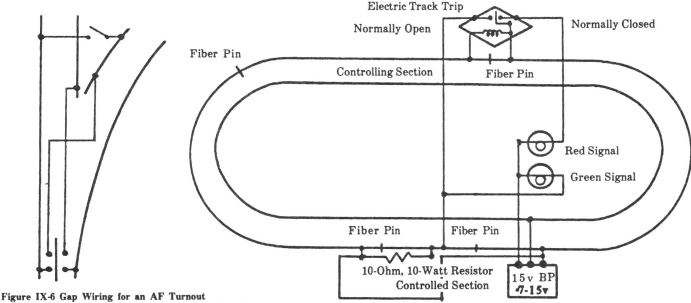

Figure IX-6 Gap Wiring for an AF Turnout
When Single Pole, Single Throw Switch is closed regular operation proceeds; when the switch is open two train operation is possible.

Figure IX-7 Wiring an Electric Track Trip

On my layout, I've set up a block and signal bridge. When the train enters the controlled section, the red light (a grain of wheat bulb) glows and the train comes to a stop.

When another train reaches the controlling section, the track trip is activated. The red light goes out, the green light goes on and the first train starts up. The wiring is illustrated here in the schematic of a simple oval layout, but you can apply the concept to any complicated pike.

In Figure IX-7 notice that the 7-15 volt side is completely intact with no fiber pins. There are a couple of different versions of the electrical trip. There is a No. 670 which attached directly to the track and had the two connectors of the switch exposed. Then there is the No. 26671 which can be connected to the track with track terminals and has only one connecting post. The 26671 must be connected using the base post as illustrated in the diagram.

ADDING ANOTHER POLE

One advantage of the No.26671 trip is the possibility of adding another pole to the switch as I have to turn on the red stop light. To add the other pole I drilled a hole on the other side of the trip, mounted a screw and soldered a flattened piece of copper wire to the screw. By adjusting the flattened wire, I was able to get contact when the trip was not activated and break contact upon activation.

The final part of any block system is a lock-out eliminator. You can use the device manufactured by American Flier or substitute a 10-ohm, 10-watt resistor which you can purchase at any radio repair or supply shop. The resistor supplies a small amount of current to the controlled section, thus keeping the reverse unit activated, but not supplying enough voltage to drive the motor in the engine.

Follow the wiring diagram and you will be able to operate two trains at the same time without the risk of a rear-end collision.

BUILD YOUR OWN TRACK TRIP FOR AC/DC

In less than an hour you can build your own track trip which will work on both Scale and AF layouts, with both an AC or DC system.

An electronic track trip is preferable to the pressure type because the latter requires that the track not be fastened down and is less reliable generally. Gilbert's track trip overcomes these obstacles, but with a large layout, you will need more trips than are available.

The electronic trip works logically: cause the current to flow through a low resistance solenoid-relay and use the relay to operate the accessories, as shown in the schematic below which identifies the proper connections. My problem in making a track trip was finding a low resistance relay. Most were far too high in resistance to run a train. If you simply placed the solenoid-relay in the circuit, the train would stall in the activation area.

The solution to this problem is to MAKE a low-resistance solenoid-relay with a glass encased reed switch and #26 magnet wire. Radio Shack sells reed switches for under $1 (for four) and the necessary parts. The track trip can be mounted on a piece of perf board one-and-one-half inches square.

WIND THE SOLENOID

Start by winding a coil of #26 enameled wire along the entire reed switch. Repeat this two more times so that the switch has three layers of wire covering it. The windings do not have to be perfectly aligned, but they should be neat. Solder one end of the coil wire to one end of the reed switch. Bend the connections on the reed switch and insert them into the perf board near the edge of the square as shown in Figure IX-8.

Next, insert the five leads from the 12-volt relay into the perf board so that the relay is located in the center of the board. Mount the 5mfd-25 volt capacitor on the opposite side of the perf board from the reed switch and at the back mount a small diode. Connect and solder the unmarked end of the diode, the negative end of the capacitor and one of the coil leads from the 12-volt relay. Trim away any excess wire.

Connect and solder the positive end of the capacitor, the other lead from the coil of the relay and the end of the reed switch that does not have the coil connected to it. Trim excess wires away. Bring the three other wires from the relay to the edge of the perf board; twist them through the holes and supply some solder to keep them neat. Your electronic track trip is ready for operation. Hook it up according to Figure IX-9.

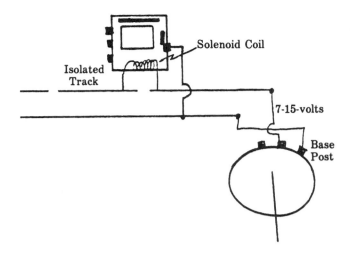

Figure IX-8 Hooking Up the Track Trip

Figure IX-9 Winding the Coil

HOW IT WORKS

When the engine passes into the activation area which should be at least 20 inches long, the current to operate the motor travels through the coil that you wound around the reed switch. This creates a magnetic field and closes the switch.

If you are using AC, the field is an alternating one and thus the reed switch chatters at 60 times a second. This chattering would cause an uneven operation for the accessory you are activating, so a diode is placed in the system to smooth out the chatter. The capacitor is charged with the pulsating DC produced by the diode and supplies an even flow to the 12-volt relay. The relay holds as long as the train draws current through the activation tracks. The 12-volt relay adds a dimension of control to the device, since it is a double-throw switch, which means that you can turn items on and off when a train passes through the activation area.

LIGHT ACTIVATED TRACK TRIP

A number of accessories are activated when the train is in a certain portion of the track. The pressure track trip is unreliable and the electrical one we just described may be a solution, but another way to get around this problem is to use a track trip that is LIGHT ACTIVATED. You can build such a device with a 6-volt relay, a Cds photocell, two transistors and two resistors. Figure IX-10 is a schematic diagram of the circuit.

To make it work, place the photocell across the track as shown in Figure IX-11 with a spotlight aiming into it. When the train passes the light, it breaks the beam and the photocell causes the current to pass through the transistors and through the relay which is used to activate the accessory. Another advantage of such a system is that in parallel track operations, the trip works on either track in either direction.

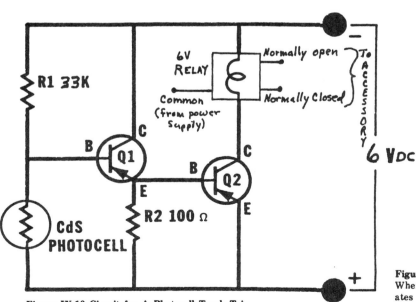

Figure IX-10 Circuit for A Photocell Track Trip
Transistors Q1 and Q2 are PNP types of moderate power handling ability. All parts are available at Radio Shack.

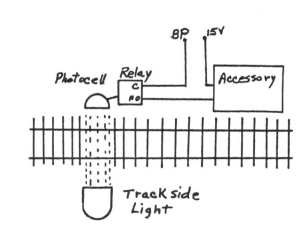

Figure IX-11 How to Use the Photocell Track Trip
When the train breaks the light beam, the relay is activated and operates the accessory. To keep room light from activating the photocell, shield the photocell with a small tube of black tape.

MY FAVORITE LAYOUTS

I like to run two trains at once, so two of my favorite layouts provide that feature. The first one requires an alert engineer. If you fall asleep at the switch you will have a certain derailment. While the setup in Figure IX-13 shows a size of 100 by 90 inches, the layout could be expanded by adding more straight track. It could also be reduced to 80 by 80 inches by removing some straight track. If it is made smaller, you will find that only small trains with a three-car consist can be run.

For the block signal in Figure IX-13, the trains BOTH run counterclockwise. Start with the first train in section 2, stopped by the block signal. Have track switch #1 (SW #1) thrown to the curved (red) and SW #2 on straight (green). You can now run the second train around the oval while the first train is waiting at the signal. But you won't want to wait all the time. So, when they are clear, throw SW #1 to straight (green) and SW #2 to curved (red). When train #2 hits section 1, it activates section 2 and train #2 starts up. Now throw SW #1 to curved and SW #2 to straight (when it is clear) and you have a running #1 train and a waiting #2 train. Remember, if you get tired, you can always leave one train running in the main loop.

Figure 14 shows a layout that could turn into a pike. It has two separate ovals, the illusion of a reverse loop and an elevated section to make use of the trestle set (that has probably been gathering dust in its box).

The only trick in wiring this fun pike is to observe the polarity (of the base post and the 7-15 volt transformer) when connecting the two ovals to the two transformers. By using two transformers — or a dual control/transformer — you gain added control over train speeds. If you use two transformers, be sure to "polarize" the connection to the wall socket. This can be done by brushing a wire that is connected to the base post of one transformer across the base post terminal of the second transformer. If you get a spark, pull the plug on the second transformer and reverse it in the socket. I then recommend that you mark the plug with paint to indicate which end is the top. This will save time when you reconnect at a later date. Have fun with you multi-train layouts.

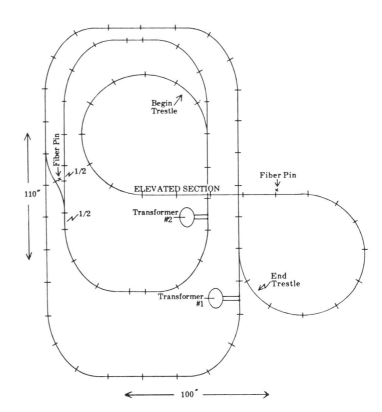

Figure IX-14 A Pike with Two Ovals and An Elevated Section

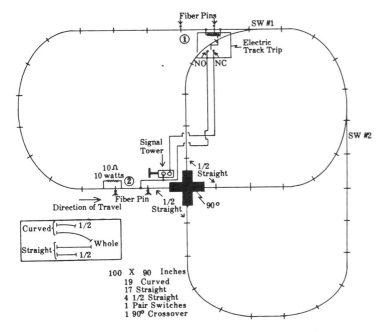

Figure IX-13   100 x 90 Inch Layout with Block Signal

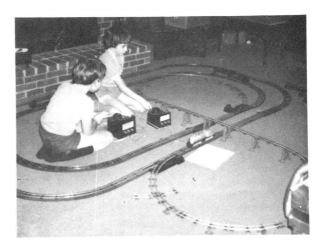

My Son Greg [in the green shorts] and His Friend Mark Play with the Layout in Figure IX-14

PARTS & SCHEMATICS APPENDIX

Nos. 283 AND 287 LOCOMOTIVE AND TENDER
WITH PISTON TYPE SMOKE AND CHOO-CHOO UNIT

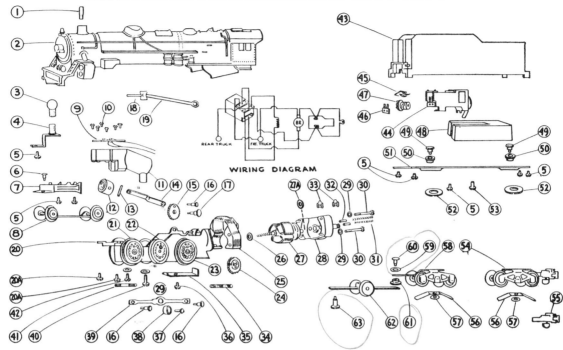

WIRING DIAGRAM

SPECIFICATIONS

Tested at: 12 Volts A.C. ....using 140'' oval of track.
(A) Motor to be tested with Remote Control Unit at 12 Volts, and not to draw more than 1.7 amps.
(B) Locomotive to run a minimum of 9 R.P.M. or 9 times forward, around 140'' oval of track per minute.
(C) Locomotive to run a minimum of 8.5. R.P.M. or 8½ times reverse, around 140'' oval of track per minute.

Load: Not to draw more than 2.1 amps. while pulling 4 Box Cars.

Motor: Universal A.C. or D.C.
Locomotive and tender with piston type smoke and choo-choo unit

6/1/60 PARTS LIST FOR #283 LOCOMOTIVE AND TENDER

No.	Description - Part Number
1	Smoke Stack - PA12A190
2	Boiler - XA11736BRP
3	Bulb - PA8999
4	Lamp Bracket Assembly - XA10890
5	Screw - S230B
	Crosshead Guide & Pilot Truck - XA10887
6	Stud - PA10707
7	Crosshead - PA10887
8	Front Truck Assembly - XA10012
	Front Truck Wheel - PA99990-A
9	Heating Element & Plate Assembly Not Available - XA10523
	Substitute with XA14A208-A
10	Screw - S183
11	Smoke Box Not Available - PA10518
	Chassis Smoke Box Assembly (Consists of Parts 9-10-11) Not Available - XA10513
	Substitute with XA13B894-RP Smoke Box Assembly
12	Piston - PA10518-A

No.	Description - Part Number
13	Piston Pin - PA10520
14	Piston Lever - PA10514
15	Worm Drive Gear - PA10671
16	Piston Rod Screw - PA7421
17	Worm Gear Stud - PA10162
18	Crosshead - PA10888
19	Connecting Rod - PA10889
20	Chassis - PA10506-A
20A	Screw - S319
21	Flanged Wheel Assembly - XA13A865
22	Flangeless Wheel & Stud - XA10009-C1
23	Pul-Mor Wheel - XA13A864
24	Worm Gear - PA10672
25	Field Assembly - XA9547-B
26	Armature Spacer - PA10766
27	Armature - XA11077
27A	Washer - W1A92
28	Brush Bracket Assembly - X9565-A

No.	Description - Part Number		No.	Description - Part Number
29	Lock Washer - PA3769		49	Truck Rivet - PA10235-A
30	Shouldered Screw - S295		50	Insulating Bushing - PA10209
31	Brush Spring - PA10757-A		51	Tender Chassis Old Style Not Available - PA12B080
32	Brush - PA9603			Substitute with PA12B080 New Style
33	Brush Cap - PA10754		52	Fiber Washer - PA8715-B
34	Worm Gear Axle Not Available -PA10006		53	Screw - S184
	Substitute with PA15A281		54	Rear Truck Assembly - XA12A050-B
35	Grease Pan - PA10017			Wheel & Axle Assembly - XA10238
36	Screw - S271			Metal Wheel - PA10140
37	Eccentric Crank Screw - PA5447			Plastic Wheel - PA9990
38	Piston Rod Spacer - PA7237			Axle - PA10238
39	Side Rod - PA9280-A		55	Knuckle Coupler - XA12A047
40	Screw - S16-C		56	Contact Spring - PA10207
41	Axle Not Available - PA10005		57	Tin Washer - PA1405
	Substitute with PA15A226		58	Front Truck Assembly Not Available - XA12A921
42	Screw - S46			Substitute with XA15A800
43	Tender Body Old Style Not Available - PA12D078-A		59	Washer - PA1067-A
	Substitute with XA12D078-CRP New Style		60	Stud - PA10751
44	Remote Control Unit - XA10587-E		61	Bushing - PA1312
45	Top Finger - XA9612-CRP		62	Coupler and Yoke Assembly Not Available - XA10749
46	Bottom Finger Unit - XA9612-BRP			Substitute with XA15A784
47	Drum - XA8716		63	Stud - PA4939
48	Tender Weight Not Available - PA11A926			
	Substitute with PA10593			

6/1/60 PARTS LIST FOR #287 LOCOMOTIVE AND TENDER

No.	Description - Part Number		No.	Description - Part Number
1	Not Used		38	Piston Rod Spacer - PA7237
2	Boiler - XA11736-ARP		39	Screw - S16C
3	Bulb - PA8999		40	Screw - S16C
4	Lamp Bracket Assembly - XA10890		41	Axle Not Available - PA10005
5	Screw - S230B			Substitute with PA15A226
	Crosshead Guide & Pilot Truck - XA10887		42	Screw - S46
6	Stud - PA10707		43	Tender Body Old Style Not Available - PA12D078A
7	Crosshead - PA10887			Substitute with XA12D078-CRP New Style
8	Front Truck Assembly - XA10012		44	Remote Control Unit - XA10587-E
	Front Truck Wheel - PA9990-A		45	Top Finger - XA9612CRP
9-17	Not Used		46	Bottom Finger Unit - XA9612-BRP
18	Crosshead - PA10888		47	Drum - XA8716
19	Connecting Rod - PA10889		48	Tender Weight Not Available - PA11A926
20	Chassis - PA10506-A			Substitute with PA10593
20A	Screw - S319		49	Truck Rivet - PA10235-A
21	Flanged Wheel Assembly - XA13A865		50	Insulating Bushing - PA10209
	Flangeless Wheel & Stud - XA10009-C1		51	Tender Chassis Old Style Not Available - PA12B080
3	Pul-Mor Wheel - XA13A864			Substitute with PA12B080 New Style
24	Worm Gear - PA10672		52	Fiber Washer - PA8715-B
25	Field Assembly - XA9547-B		53	Screw - S184
26	Armature Spacer - PA10766		54	Rear Truck Assembly - XA12A050-B
27	Armature - XA11077			Wheel and Axle Assembly - XA10238
27A	Washer - W1A92			Metal Wheel - PA10140
28	Brush Bracket Assembly - XA9565-A			Plastic Wheel - PA9990
29	Lock Washer - PA3769			Axle - PA10238
30	Shouldered Screw - S295		55	Knuckle Coupler - XA12A047
31	Brush Spring - PA10757-A		56	Contact Spring - PA10207
32	Brush - PA9603		57	Tin Washer - PA1405
33	Brush Cap - PA10754		58	Front Truck Assembly Not Available - XA12A921
34	Worm Gear Axle Not Available - PA10006			Substitute with XA15A800
	Substitute with PA15A281		59	Washer - PA1067-A
35	Grease Pan - PA10017		60	Stud - PA10751
36	Screw - S271		61	Bushing - PA1312
37	Eccentric Crank Screw - PA5447		62	Coupler and Yoke Assembly Not Available - XA10749
				Substitute with XA15A784
			63	Stud - PA4939

No. 293 LOCOMOTIVE AND TENDER
WITH PISTON TYPE SMOKE AND CHOO-CHOO UNIT AND PULL-MOR

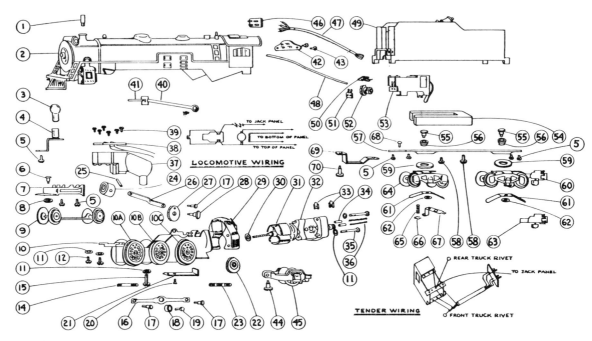

SPECIFICATIONS

Tested at: 12 Volts A.C. ....using 140'' oval of track.
(A) Motor to be tested with Remote Control Unit at 12 Volts, and not to draw more than 1.7 amps.
(B) Locomotive to run a minimum of 9 R.P.M. or 9 times forward, around 140'' oval of track per minute.
(C) Locomotive to run a minimum of 8.5 R.P.M. or 8½ times reverse, around 140'' oval of track per minute.

Load: Not to draw more than 2.1 amps. while pulling 4 Box Cars.
Motor: Universal A.C. or D.C.
Locomotive and tender with piston type smoke and choo-choo unit and pull-mor

6/1/60 PARTS LIST FOR #293 LOCOMOTIVE AND TENDER

No.	Description - Part No.
1	Smoke Stack - PA12A190
2	Boiler Assembly - XA10A886-D
3	Bulb - PA8999
4	Lamp Bracket - XA10890
5	Screw - S230-B
	Crosshead Guide & Pilot Truck Assembly (consists of parts 6-7-8-9) - XA10887
6	Stud - PA10707
7	Crosshead Guide - PA10887
8	Washer - PA5035-A
9	Front Truck Assembly - XA10012
	Front Truck Wheel only - PA9990-A
10	Chassis - PA10506
10A	Flanged Wheel with Tapped Hole - XA12A449
10B	Flangeless Wheel and Stud - XA10009-C1
10C	Pul Mor Wheel - XA12A447
11	Washer - PA3769
12	Screw - S14
13	Screw - S14
14	Plain Axle - PA10005
15	Screw - S16-C
16	Side Rod - PA9280-A
17	Screw - PA7421
18	Piston Rod Spacer - PA7237
19	Screw - PA5447
20	Screw - S271
21	Grease Pan - PA10017
22	Worm Gear (Motor) - PA10672
23	Worm Gear Axle - PA10006
	Piston & Lever Assembly (consists of parts 24-25-26) - XA10514
24	Piston - PA10518-A
25	Piston Pin - PA10520
26	Piston Lever - PA10514
27	Worm Gear Smoke Drive - PA10671
28	Worm Gear Stud - PA10162
29	Magnet Assembly A.C. - XA9547
30	Washer - PA10766
31	Armature Assembly A.C. - XA11077
32	Brush Bracket Assembly - XA9565-A
33	Brush Cap - PA10754
34	Carbon Brush A.C. - PA9603
35	Screw - S295
36	Brush Spring - PA10757-A
	Chassis Smoke Box Assembly (consists of parts 37-38-39)
37	Chassis Smoke Box - PA10513

38	Heating Element & Plate Assembly - XA10523		55	Truck Rivet - PA10235-A
39	Screw - S183		56	Insulating Bushing - PA10290
40	Connecting Rod - PA10889		57	Tender Chassis - PA12B080
41	Crosshead - PA10888		58	Screw - S184
42	Jack Panel - XA10662-A		59	Washer - PA8715-B
43	Screw - S222		60	Rear Truck Assembly - XA12A350
44	Truck Stud - PA4939		61	Contact Spring - PA10207
45	Rear Truck Assembly - XA10020		62	Washer - PA1405
46	Male Plug - XA10663		63	Knuckle Coupler - XA12A047
47	4 Conductor Cable - PA10511-C		64	Front Truck Assembly - XA12A516
48	9"Lead Wire - PA10249-T		65	Spring - PA11A956
49	Tender Body Assembly with Trimmings - XA12A081RP		66	Hair Pin Cotter - PA11A944
50	Top Finger Unit (Remote Control) - XA9612-C		67	Tender Pick-Up - PA11A936
51	Bottom Finger Unit (Remote Control) - XA9612-B		68	Rivet - PA4366
52	Drum (Remote Control) - XA8716		69	Coupler Strap - PA12A520
53	Remote Control Unit - XA10587-E		70	Screw - PA4938
54	Tender Weight - PA11A926			

10/1/62 REVISIONS FOR #293 LOCOMOTIVE AND TENDER

Changes only listed below:

No.	Description - Part No.			
2	Boiler Assembly - XA10A886-DRP		38	Heating Element & Plate Assembly - XA14A208-A
10	Chassis - PA10506-A		43	Screw - S230-B
10A	Flanged Wheel - XA13A865		45	Truck Assembly - XA15A261
10B	Flangeless Wheel and Stud - XA10009-C1			Substitute for XA10020
10C	Pul Mor Wheel - XA13A864		47	4 Conductor Cable (plastic) - PA13A208-A
14	Plain Axle - PA15A226		48	Lead Wire - PA10249
23	Worm Gear Axle - PA15A281		50	Top Finger Unit (Remote Control) - XA9612-CRP
37	Smoke Box Assembly - XA1313894RP		51	Bottom Finger Unit (Remote Control) - XA9612-BRP
			54	Tender Weight - PA10593
			57	Tender Chassis - No Longer Available

No. 303 LOCOMOTIVE AND TENDER
WITH PISTON TYPE SMOKE AND CHOO-CHOO UNIT,
PULL-MOR WHEELS AND KNUCKLE COUPLER

SPECIFICATIONS

Tested at: 12 Volts A.C. ....using 140'' oval of track.
(A) Motor to be tested with Remote Control Unit at 12 Volts, and not to draw more than .175 amps.
(B) Locomotive to run a minimum of 9 R.P.M. or 9 times forward, around 140'' oval of track per minute.
(C) Locomotive to run a minimum of 8.5 R.P.M. or 8½ times reverse, around 140'' oval of track per minute.

Load: Not to draw more than 2 amps. while pulling 4 Box Cars.

Motor: Universal A.C. or D.C.
Locomotive and tender with piston type smoke and choo-choo unit, pull-mor wheels and knuckle coupler

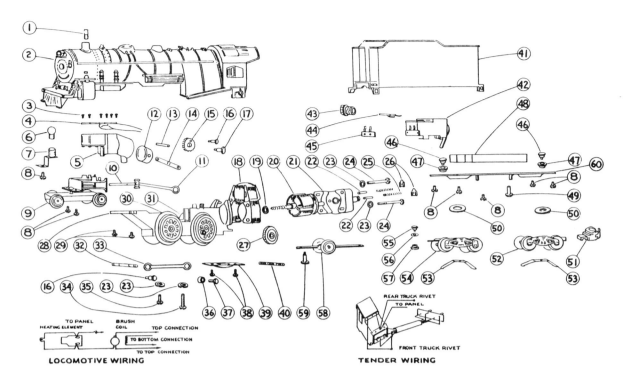

LOCOMOTIVE WIRING

TENDER WIRING

6/1/60 PARTS LIST FOR #303 LOCOMOTIVE AND TENDER

No.	Description - Part No.
1	Smoke Stack - PA12A190
2	Boiler Assembly - XA11A975-BRP
	Headlight Lens - PA10542
	Motor Mount - PA9286
	Screw #2 x 1/4" Type "Z" P.K. - S183
	Smoke Box Assembly - XA10513
	Not Available - Substitute with XA13B894RP -
4	Heating Element & Plate Assembly - XA10523
	Not Available - Substitute with XA14A208
5	Smoke Box - PA10513
	Not Available - Substitute with PA13B894
	Separator - PA14A209
6	Bulb - PA8999
7	Lamp Bracket Assembly - XA10890
8	Screw #4 x 1/4' Type 'Z' P.K. - S230-B
9	Guide & Truck Assembly - XA13A085
	Crosshead Guide - PA10887
	Pilot Truck - XA13A084
	Rivet - PA4367
10	Crosshead - PA11099
11	Connecting Rod - PA10889
12	Piston - PA10518-A
13	Piston Pin - PA10520
14	Piston Lever - PA10517
15	Worm Gear - PA10671
16	Screw - PA7421
17	Worm Gear Stud - PA10162
18	Magnet Assembly - XA9547
19	Armature Spacer - PA10766
20	Armature Assembly - XA11077
21	Brush Bracket Assembly - XA9565-A
22	Brush - PA9603
23	Washer - PA3769
24	Screw #6-32 x 1 7/32" Shouldered - S295
25	Brush Spring - PA10757-A
26	Brush Cap - PA10754
27	Worm Gear (motor) - PA10672

No.	Description - Part No.
28	Chassis - PA10512
29	Screw #6 x 5/16" Type "Z" P.K. - S319
30	Flanged Wheel Assembly - XA13A865
31	Pul Mor Wheel & Stud Assembly - XA13A866
32	Plain Axle - PA10005 - Not Available - Substitute with PA15A226
33	Side Rod - PA9452
34	Screw #6-32 x 3/4" R.H. - S18
35	Screw - S16C
36	Piston Rod Spacer - PA7237
37	Screw - PA5447
38	Screw #4 x l/4" Type "Z" P.K. - S230-B
39	Motor Cover Plate - PA10080
40	Worm Gear Axle - PA10006
	Not Available - Substitute with PA15A281
41	Tender Body - PA12D078
	Not Available - Substitute with PA12D078 New Style
42	Remote Control Unit - XA10587-E43 Drum Only - XA8716
44	Top Finger Unit - XA9612-CRP
45	Bottom Finger Unit - XA9612-BRP
46	Truck Rivet - PA10235-A
47	Insulating Bushing - PA10209
48	Tender Weight - PA11A926
	Not Available - Substitute with PA10593
49	Screw - S184
50	Washer - PA8715-B
51	Knuckle Coupler - XA12A047
52	Rear Truck Assembly - XA12A050-B
	Wheel & Axle Assembly - XA10238
	Brass Wheel - PA10140
	Plastic Wheel - PA9990
	Axle - PA10238
53	Contact Spring - PA10207
54	Front Truck Assembly - XA14A349
	Not Available - Substitute with XA15A80
55	Stud - PA14A346*
56	Washer - PA1067-A*
57	Insulating Bushing - PA14A347*

58   Coupler & Yoke Assembly - XA10749
      Not Available - Substitute with Draw Bar Assembly
59   Screw - PA4939
60   Tender Chassis - XA12B080
      Not Available - Substitute with PA12B080 New Style

* Part # 55-56-57 not used with # 54 - XA15A800 Truck or # 58 - XA15A784 Draw Bar Assembly.

10/62 REVISIONS FOR #303 LOCOMOTIVE AND TENDER

Changes only listed below:

No.	Description - Part No.
2	Boiler Assembly Marked 21105 - XA11A975ERP
	Left Motor Mount - PA16052
	Right Motor Mount - PA16053
4	Heating Element & Plate Assembly - XA14A208-A
5	Smoke Box - XA13B894RP
32	Plain Axle - PA15A226

40	Worm Gear Axle - PA15A281
41	Tender Body - No Longer Available - No Substitute
48	Tender Weight - PA10593
54	Front Truck Assembly - XA15A800 Substitute for XA14A34
58	Draw Bar Assembly - XA15A784
	Used only on XA15B800 Truck Assembly
	Coupler & Yoke Assembly - XA10891
60	Tender Chassis - Obsolete - No Longer Available

No. 315 PENNSYLVANIA K5 LOCOMOTIVE AND TENDER
WITH SMOKE CHOO-CHOO AND AIR CHIME WHISTLE

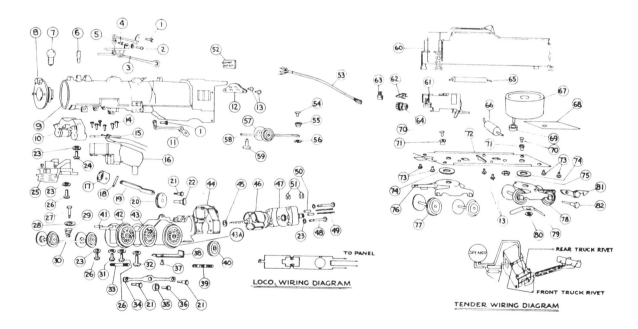

LOCO. WIRING DIAGRAM

TENDER WIRING DIAGRAM

SPECIFICATIONS

Tested at: 12 Volts A.C. ....using 140'' oval track.
      (A) Motor to be tested with Remote Control at 12 Volts and not to draw more than 1.7 amps.
      (B) Locomotive and tender to run a minimum of 9 R.P.M. or 9 times forward around 140'' oval of track per minute pulling 4 cars.

      (C) Locomotive and tender to run a minimum of 8.5 R.P.M. or 8½ times reverse around 140'' oval of track per minute pulling 4 cars.

Load: Not to draw more than 2.1 amps. while pulling 4 Box Cars.

Motor: Universal A.C. or D.C.
      Pennsylvania K5 locomotive and tender with smoke, choo-choo and air chime whistle

6/1/60 PARTS LIST FOR #315 PENN K5 LOCOMOTIVE AND TENDER WITH SMOKE, CHOO-CHOO AND AIR CHIME WHISTLE

No.	Description - Part No.
1	Link Stud - PA10598
2	Screw - S-1
3	Washer - W-46
4	Shouldered Screw - PA9288
5	Crosshead Assembly (Right) - XA10668-R
	Crosshead Assembly (Left) - XA10668-L
6	Smoke Stack - PA12A190
7	14 Volt Lamp - PA8999
8	Boiler Front Assembly - XA9504-DRP
	Headlight Lens - PA10542
9	Boiler Assembly - XA9423-F
	Mounting Bracket (Rear) - PA9579
	Coupler Strap - XA9578
10	Cylinder - PA10018
11	Eccentric Crank Assembly - XA10447
12	Jack Panel - XA10662
13	Screw - S230-B
14	Screw - S183
15	Heating Element & Plate Assembly - XA10523
	Not Available - Substitute with XA14A208
16	Smoke Box Assembly - XA10513
	Not Available - Substitute with XA13B894-RP
	Smoke Box - PA10513
	Not Available - Substitute with PA23B894
	Separator (not shown) - PA14A209
17	Piston - PA10518-A
18	Piston Pin - PA10520
19	Piston Lever - PA10514
20	Worm Gear (Smoke Drive) - PA10671
21	Screw - PA7421
22	Worm Gear Stud - PA10162
23	Washer - PA3769
24	Screw - S-16
25	Pilot - PA9502
26	Screw - S-46
27	Front Truck Stud - PA10707
28	Front Truck Washer - W-6
29	Front Truck Spring - PA8887
30	Front Truck - XA10012
	Axle - PA13A082
	Plastic Wheel - PA9990
	Front Truck & Pilot Assembly
	(Consists of Parts 25-27-28-29-30) - XA9502-C
31	Screw - S-14
32	Not Used
33	Plain Axle - PA10005
	Not Available - Substitute with PA15A226
34	Side Rod - PA9280-A
35	Piston Rod Spacer - PA7237
36	Screw - PA5447
37	Screw - S271
38	Grease Pan - PA10017
39	Worm Gear Axle - PA10006
	Not Available - Substitute with PA15A281
40	Worm Gear (Motor) - PA10672
41	Chassis Assembly with Bearings only - XA10506
	Bearing - PA13A187
42	Flanged Drive Wheel - XA13A865
43	Flangeless Drive Wheel with Stud - XA10009-B1

No.	Description - Part No.
43A	Pul Mor Wheel Assembly - XA13A864
44	Field Assembly - XA9547
45	Armature Spacer - PA10766
46	Armature Assembly - XA11077
47	Brush Bracket Assembly - XA9565-A
48	Screw - S295
49	Brush Spring - PA10757-A
50	Brush - PA9603
51	Brush Cap - PA10754
52	Male Plug - XA10663
53	4 Conductor Cable - PA10511
54	Stud - PA10751
55	Fiber Bushing - PA1312
56	Washer - PA1067-A
57	Rear Truck Wheel Only - PA10019-A
58	Coupler & Yoke Assembly - Not Available - XA10749*
59	Screw - PA4938
60	Tender Body Assembly with Trimmings - XA9667-RP
61	Remote Control Unit - XA10587-E
62	Top Finger Unit - XA9612-CRP
63	Bottom Finger Unit - XA9612-BRP
64	Drum - XA8716
65	Resistor - PA11685
66	Condenser - PA11A991
	Not Available - Substitute with PA14A914
67	Speaker - XA11710
	Not Available - Substitute with XA14A127
	Speaker Bracket - PA14A216
	Screw - S230-B
	Screw - S171
68	Not Used
69	Not Used
70	Truck Rivet - PA10235-A
71	Insulating Bushing - PA10209
72	Chassis & Wire Retainer Assembly - XA10588
73	Screw - S-0
74	Insulating Washer - PA8715-B
75	Not Used
76	Front Truck Assembly - Not Available - XA11712*
77	Wheel & Axle Assembly - XA10238
	Metal Wheel Only - PA10140
	Plastic Wheel Only - PA9990
	Axle Only - PA10238
78	Rear Truck Assembly - Not Available - XA11714*
79	Contact Spring - PA10207
80	Washer - PA1405
81	Coupler and Weight Assembly - XA10469
	Coupler Weight Only - Not Available - PA10692
82	Coupler Pin - Not Available - PA10467

Link Couplers & Trucks not available, convert to knuckle couplers by using:

58	Coupler & Yoke Assembly XA15A784
76	Front Truck Assembly - XA14B811
	Hair Pin Cotter - PA11A944
	Spring - PA11A956
	Tender Pick Up - PA11A936
78	Rear Truck Assembly
	plus parts listed under 76 - XA12A350
	Coupler Strap (Connects Loco & Tender) - PA14A839

Changes only listed below:

No.	Description - Part No.
9	Boiler Assembly - XA9423-JRP
15	Heating Element & Plate Assembly - XA14A208-A
16	Smoke Box Assembly - XA13B894-RP*
25	Pilot with Truck - XA9502D
33	Plain Axle - PA15A226
39	Worm Gear Axle - PA15A281
41	Chassis Assembly with Bearings only - PA10506-A
53	4 Conductor Cable - plastic - PA13208-A
58	Draw Bar Assembly - XA15A784
	Used with XA14B811 Front Truck Assembly

	Coupler & Yoke Assembly - XA10891
	Substitute for XA10749
66	Condenser - PA14A914 - Substitute for PA11A991
67	Speaker- XA14A127 Conv. - Substitute for XA11710
76	Front Truck Assembly- XA14B811 - Substitute for XA11712
	Hair Pin Cotter - PA11A944
	Spring - PA11A956
	Tender Pick Up - PA11A936
78	Rear Truck Assembly - XA12A350
	Substitute for XA11714- -Plus Parts listed under Diagram 76

* #16 When using XA13B894-RP remove Screw on Solder Terminal

No. 326 AMERICAN FLYER LOCOMOTIVE AND TENDER
WITH SMOKE, CHOO-CHOO, AIR CHIME WHISTLE AND PULL-MOR

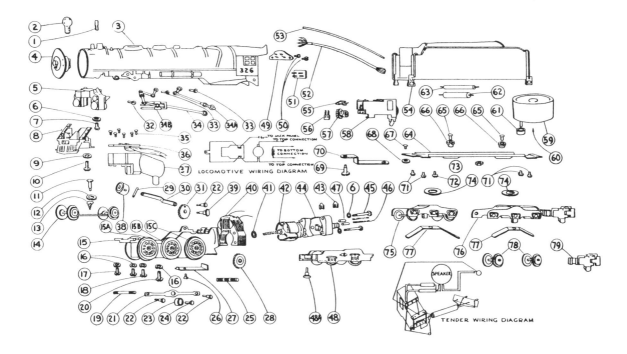

SPECIFICATIONS

Tested at: 12 Volts A.C. ....using 140'' oval of track.
(A) Motor to be tested with Remote Control Unit at 12 Volts, and not to draw more than .175 amps.
(B) Locomotive to run a minimum of 9 R.P.M. or 9 times forward, around 140'' oval of track per minute.
(C) Locomotive to run a minimum of 8.5 R.P.M. or 8½ times reverse, around 140'' oval of track per minute.

Load: Not to draw more than 2.1 amps. while pulling 4 Box Cars.

Motor: Universal A.C. or D.C.
American Flyer locomotive and tender with smoke, choo-choo, air chime whistle and pull-mor

No.	Description - Part Number
1	Smoke Stack - PA12A190
2	14 Volt Lamp - PA8999
3	Boiler Assembly - XA11A939-RP
	Crossbar - XA9578
	Motor Mount - PA9579
4	Boiler Front Assembly with Lamp Bracket - XA9216-B
	Headlight Lens - PA10542
5	Cylinder and Steamchest - PA10056
6	Lockwasher - PA3769
7	Screw - S47
8	Pilot - PA9245
9	Lockwasher - PA3769
10	Screw
11	Front Truck Stud - PA10707
12	Washer - W6
13	Front Truck Spring - PA8887
14	Front Truck - XA10012
	Front Truck Wheel Only - PA9900-A
15	Chassis Assembly - PA10506-A
15A	Flanged Wheel - XA13A865
15B	Flangeless Wheel and Stud - XA10009-B1
15C	Pul Mor Wheel - XA13A864
16	Lockwasher - PA3769
17	Screw - S14
18	Screw - S46
19	Plain Axle - PA10005 - Not Available
	Substitute with PA15A226
20	Not Used
21	Side Rod - PA9280-A
22	Screw PA7421
23	Spacer for Piston Rod - PA7237
24	Screw - PA5447
25	Worm Gear Axle - PA10006 - Not Available
	Substitute with PA15A281
26	Screw - S271
27	Grease Pan - PA10017
28	Worm Gear (Motor) - PA10672
29	Piston Pin - PA10520
30	Piston Lever - PA10514
31	Worm Gear (Smoke Drive) - PA10671
32	Screw - PA9288
33	Link Stud - PA10598
34	Crosshead Assembly (Right) - XA10597-R
	Crosshead Assembly (Left) - XA10597-L
34A	Eccentric Crank Assembly - XA10447-A
34B	Crosshead Guide (Right) - PA10595-R
	Crosshead Guide (Left) - PA10595-L
35	Screw - S183
36	Heating Element & Plate Assembly - XA10523 - Not Available
	Substitute with XA14A208A
37	Smoke Box Assembly - XA10513 - Not Available
	Substitute with XA13B894-RP
	Smoke Box - PA10513 - Not Available
	Substitute with PA13B894
	Separator - PA14A209

No.	Description - Part Number
38	Piston - PA10518-A
39	Worm Gear Stud - PA10162
40	Magnet Assembly - XA12A526
41	Washer - PA10766
42	Armature Assembly - XA12A523
43	Brush Cap - PA10754
44	Brush Bracket Assembly - XA9565-A
45	Screw - S3A78 - Not Available
	Substitute with S29
46	Brush Spring - PA10757-A
47	Carbon brush - PA9603
48	Rear Truck Assembly - XA10002 - Not Available
	Substitute with XA14B837
48A	Rear Truck Stud - PA4938
49	Jack Panel - XA10662-A
50	Screw - S222
51	Male Plug - XA10663
52	4 Conductor Cable - PA10511
53	7 1/2" Lead Wire - P9273
54	Tender Body with Trimmings - XA9312-RP
55	Top Finger Unit - XA9612-CRP
56	Bottom Finger Unit - XA9612-BRP
57	Drum - XA8716
58	Remote Control Unit - XA10587-E
59	Speaker - XA11710 - Not Available
	Speaker - XA11B831 - Not Available
	Substitute with XA14A127
	Speaker Bracket for XA14A127 - PA14A216
	Screw for XA14A12 Speaker - S171
	4.3/16 B.D.H.D. Type "Z" P.K. Screw for XA14A127 Speaker - S172
60	Not Used
61	Not Used
62	Condenser - PA11A991 - Not Available
	Substitute with PA14A914
63	Resistor - PA11685
64	Chassis & Wire Retainer Assembly - XA10582-A
65	Truck Rivet - PA10235-A
66	Insulating Bushing - PA10209
67	Tubular Rivet - PA4366
68	Washer - W79
69	Stud - PA4939
70	Coupler - PA10244
71	Screw - S-O
72	Screw - S230B
73	Not Used
74	Washer - PA8715-B
75	Front Truck Assembly with Wheels - XA11A909
76	Rear Truck Assembly with Wheels - XA12A053
77	Contact Spring - PA10241
78	Wheel & Axle Assembly (metal and plastic wheels) - XA10238
	Plastic Wheel - PA9990
	Metal Wheel - PA10140
	Axle - PA10238
79	Knuckler Coupler - XA12A047

10/1/62 PARTS REVISIONS FOR #326 LOCOMOTIVE AND TENDER

Changes only listed below:

No.	Description - Part Number
3	Boiler Assembly (Marked 21130) - XA11A939-CRP
19	Plain Axle - PA15A226
25	Worm Gear Axle - PA15A281
36	Heating Element & Plate Assembly - XA14A208-A
37	Smoke Box Assembly - XA13B894-RP*
45	Screw - S29

No.	Description - Part Number
48	Rear Truck Assembly - XA14B837
52	4 Conductor Wire (Plastic) - PA13208-A
59	Speaker - XA14A127-Conv.
	Substitute for XA11710 & XA11B831

* #37 When using XA13B894-RP remove Screw on Solder Terminal.

No. 336 U.P. LOCOMOTIVE AND TENDER
WITH SMOKE, CHOO-CHOO, AIR CHIME WHISTLE AND PULL-MOR

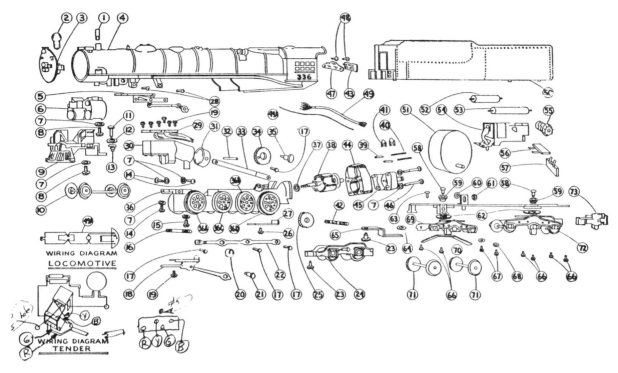

WIRING DIAGRAM LOCOMOTIVE

WIRING DIAGRAM TENDER

SPECIFICATIONS

Tested at: 12 Volts A.C. ....using 140'' oval of track.
Not to draw more than 1.3 amps.
(A) Locomotive to a run a minimum of 11 R.P.M. or 11 times forward, around 140'' oval of track per minute.
(B) Locomotive to run a minimum of 10 R.P.M. or 10 times in reverse, around 140'' oval of track per minute.

Load: Not to draw more than 2 amps. while pulling 4 Box or Cattle Cars.

Motor: Universal A.C. or D.C.
U.P. locomotive and tender with smoke, choo-choo, air chime whistle and pull-mor

6/1/60 PARTS LIST FOR #336 U. P. LOCOMOTIVE & TENDER

No.	Description - Part Number
1	Smoke Stack - PA12A190
2	14 Volt Lamp - PA8999
3	Boiler Front Assembly with Lamp Socket - XA8960-C
	Headlight Lens - PA10542
4	Boiler Assembly - XA8956-L
	Mounting Bracket - PA9579
	Coupler Strap Assembly - XA9578
5	Valve Link Assembly (Right or Left) - XA10057-R or L
6	Cylinder & Steamchest - PA10030
7	Lockwasher - PA3769
8	Screw - S-16
	Pilot & Front Truck Assembly (consists of parts 9-13) - XA8959-A
9	Pilot - PA8959
10	Front Truck - XA10012
	Front Truck Wheel Only - PA9990
11	Stud - PA13A404
12	Washer - W-6
13	Front Truck Spring - PA8887
14	Screw - S46
15	Screw - S18
16	Plain Axle - PA10005 - Not Available
	Substitute with PA15A226
17	Screw - PA7421

No.	Description - Part Number
18	Crosshead Assembly - XA10669RA
	Crosshead Assembly - XA10669LA
19	Screw - S183
20	Piston Rod Spacer - PA7237
21	Screw - PA5447
22	Side Rod - PA8994-A
23	Stud - PA4938
24	Rear Truck Assembly - XA10002 - Not Available
	Substitute with XA14B837
25	Worm Gear (Motor) - PA10672
26	Screw - S271
27	Grease Pan - PA10017A
28	Screw - S171
29	Heating Element & Plate Assembly - XA10523 - Not Available
	Substitute with XA14A208A
30	Chassis Smoke Box Assembly - XA10513 - Not Available
	Substitute with XA13B894RP
	Smoke Box - PA10513
	Not Available - Substitute with PA13B894
	Separator - PA14A209
31	Piston - PA10518-A
32	Piston Pin - PA10520
33	Piston Lever - PA10515
34	Worm Gear (Smoke Drive) - PA10671

35	Worm Gear Stud - PA10162
36	Chassis with Bushings - XA10505
36A	Flanged Wheel Assembly - XA13A861
36B	Flangeless Wheel Assembly with Tapped Hole - XA10010-A
36C	Flangeless Wheel Assembly with Stud - XA10010-A3
36D	Pul Mor Wheel - XA13A863
37	Washer - PA 10766
38	Armature Assembly - XA12A523
39	Carbon Brush - PA9603
40	Brush Spring - PA10757-A
41	Brush Cap - PA10754
42	Worm Gear Axle - PA10006 - Not Available
	Substitute with PA15A281
43	Male Plug - XA10663
44	Magnet Assembly - XA12A526
45	Brush Bracket Assembly - X49565-A
46	Screw - S3A78 - Not Available
	Substitute with S29
47	Jack Panel - XA10662
48	Screw - S230-B
49	4 Conductor Cable - PA10511
49A	10 1/2" Lead Wire - PA10249
50	Tender Body Assembly with Trimmings - XA8914RP
	Tender Chassis - PA10591-A
51	Speaker - XA11710 - Not Available
	Speaker - XA11B831 - Not Available
	Substitute with XA14A127
	Mounting Bracket - PA14A216
	Screw - S171
	Screw - S230B

52	Condenser - PA11A991 - Not Available
	Substitute with PA14A914
53	Resistor - PA11685
54	Remote Control Unit - XA10587-E
	Screw (Remote Control Unit) - S230B
55	Drum - XA8716
56	Top Finger Unit - XA9612-CRP
57	Bottom Finger Unit - XA9612-BRP
58	Rivet - PA9988
59	Fiber Bushing - PA10240
60	Not Used
61	Not Used
62	Washer - PA8715-B
63	Rivet - P4652
64	Washer - W79
65	Coupler Bar - PA10239
66	Screw - S-1
67	Not Used
68	Not Used
69	Front Truck with Wheels - XA11A909
70	Contact Spring - PA10241
71	Wheel and Axle Assembly - XA10238
	Metal Wheel - PA10140
	Plastic Wheel - PA9990
	Axle - PA10238
72	Rear Truck with Wheels - XA12A053
	Shoe - PA11677-A
	Spring - PA11533
73	Knuckle Coupler - XA12A047

10/1/62 PARTS REVISIONS FOR #336 LOCOMOTIVE & TENDER

Changes only listed below:

No.	Description - Part Number
16	Plain Axle - PA15A226
24	Rear Truck Assembly - XA14B837
29	Heating Element & Plate Assembly - XA14A208A
30	Smoke Box Assembly - XA13B894RP*
42	Worm Gear Axle - PA15A281

46	Screw - S29
47	Jack Panel - XA10662-A
49	4 Conductor Cable (Plastic) - PA13A208A
51	Speaker - XA14A127
	Substitute for XA11710 & XA11B831
52	Condenser - PA14A914
	Substitute for PA11A991

NO. 343 LOCOMOTIVE AND TENDER WITH SMOKE
AND CHOO-CHOO UNIT, PULL-MOR WHEELS,
KNUCKLE COUPLER

SPECIFICATIONS

Tested at: 12 Volts A.C. ....using 140'' oval of track.
(A) Motor to be tested with Remote Control Unit at 12 Volts and not to draw more than 1.55 amps.
(B) Locomotive to run at a minimum of 9 R.P.M. or 9 times forward around 140'' oval of track per minute.
(C) Locomotive to run at a minumum of 8.5 R.P.M. or 8½ times reverse around 140'' oval of track per minute.

Load: Not to draw more than 2.1 amps. while pulling 4 Box Cars.
Motor: Universal A.C. or D.C.
Locomotive and tender with smoke and choo-choo unit, Pull-Mor wheels, knuckle coupler

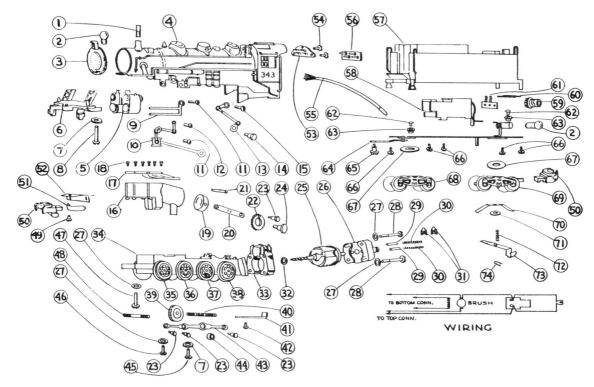

6/1/60 PARTS LIST FOR #343 LOCOMOTIVE AND TENDER

No.	Description - Part Number
1	Smoke Stack - PA12A190
2	14 Volt Lamp - PA8999
3	Boiler Front - XA9467-B
	Headlight Lens - PA10543
4	Boiler Assembly - XA9466-CRP
	Motor Mount - PA9286-A
5	Cylinder - PA10109
6	Pilot - PA12C478
7	Lock Washer - P4654
8	Screw - S55
9	Crosshead Guide (right or left) - PA10595 R & L
10	Crosshead Assembly (right or left) - XA10596 R & L
11	Screw - S-1
12	Link Stud - PA10598
13	Eccentric Crank - XA10447-B
14	Eccentric Crank Screw - PA5447
15	Shouldered Screw - PA9288
16	Smoke Box Assembly - XA10513 - Not Available
	Substitute with XA13B894-RP
	Smoke Box - PA10513 - Not Available
	Substitute with PA13B894
	Separator - PA14A209
17	Heating Element & Plate Assembly - XA10523 - Not Available
	Substitute with XA14A208-A
18	Screw - S183
19	Piston - PA105l8-A
20	Piston Lever - PA10516
21	Piston Pin - PA10520
22	Worm Gear - PA10671
23	Screw - PA7421
24	Worm Gear Stud - PA10162
25	Armature - XA11077
26	Brush Bracket - XA9565-A
27	Lock Washer - PA3769
28	Screw - S295
29	Brush - PA9603
30	Brush Spring - PA10757-A
31	Brush Cap - PA10754
32	Armature Spacer - PA10766
33	Field Assembly - XA9547
34	Chassis with bushing - XA10504
35	Flanged Wheel - XA12A472
36	Flangeless Wheel - XA10104-B
37	Flangeless Wheel with Stud - XA10104-A2
38	Pul Mor Wheel - XA12A473
39	Worm Gear - PA9473
40	Worm Gear Axle - PA10006 - Not Available
	Substitute with PA15A281
41	Grease Pan - PA10017
42	Screw - S271
43	Side Rod - PA9476
44	Piston Rod Spacer - PA7237
45	Screw - S16-C
46	Screw - S24
47	Screw - S52
48	Axle - PA10005 - Not Available
	Substitute with PA15A226
49	Screw - S3A71
50	Knuckle Coupler - XA12A047
51	Leaf Spring - PA12A355-A
52	Coupler Ratchet - PA12A479-A
53	Jack Panel - XA10662-A
54	Screw - S230-B
55	4 Conductor Cable - PA10511
56	Male Plug Assembly - XA10663
57	Tender Body - XA9778-BRP
58	Remote Control - XA10587-E
59	Drum - XA8716
60	Top Finger Unit - XA9612-CRP
61	Bottom Finger Unit - XA9612-BRP
62	Coupler Rivet - PA10235-A
63	Insulating Bushing - PA10209
64	Chassis - XA10592
65	Stud - PA4938
66	Screw - S-O

67	Fiber Washer - PA8715-B		71	Tin Washer - PA1405
68	Front Truck Assembly - XA12A516		72	Spring - PA11A956
69	Rear Truck Assembly - XA12A350		73	Tender Pickup - PA11A936
	Wheel & Axle Assembly - XA10238		74	Hair Pin Cotter - PA11A944
	Wheel - PA9990			**Not Shown**
	Axle - PA10238			Black Lead Wire - LW-1B1
	Wheel - PA10140			Armature Washer (front) - W1A92
70	Contact Spring - PA10207			

10/1/62 PARTS REVISIONS FOR #343 LOCOMOTIVE AND TENDER

Changes only listed below:

No.	Description - Part Number		No.	Description - Part Number
16	Smoke Box - XA13B894RP*		40	Worm Gear Axle - PA15A281
17	Heating Element & Plate Assembly - XA14A208-A		48	Plain Axle - PA15A226
			55	4 Conductor Cable (plastic) - PA13A208A

No. 372
UNION PACIFIC GP-7 DIESEL

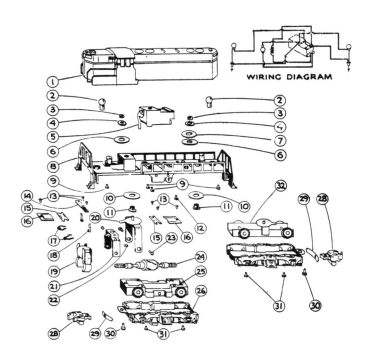

WIRING DIAGRAM

SPECIFICATIONS

Tested at: 12 Volts A.C. ....using 160'' oval of track.
(A) Diesel to pull 4 cars and run a minimum of 9 R.P.M. or 9 times forward or reverse around 160'' oval of track.

Load: Not to draw more than 1.8 amps. while pulling 4 cars.

Motor: Universal A.C. or D.C.

6/1/60 PARTS FOR 370 NOT AVAILABLE
PARTS FOR 371 & 372 UNION PACIFIC DIESEL

No.	Description - Part Number
1	Body - XA11384-BRP
2	Bulb - PA8999
3	Tru-arc Ring - P10800-A
4	Washer - W83
5	Remote Control Unit - XA10587-E
	Drum - XA8716
	Bottom Finger Unit - XA9612-BRP
	Top Finger Unit - XA9612-CRP
6	Washer - W124
7	Steel Washer - W126
8	Chassis & Lamp Bracket Assembly - XA14A094-A
	End Rail - XA11B913-RP
9	Screw - S4N30
10	Fiber Washer - PA8715
11	Fiber Bushing - PA11455
12	Screw - S230B
13	Screw - S171
14	Mounting Bracket - XA11454-RP
15	Bearing Strap - PA11453
16	Worm Cover - PA11441
17	Brush Springs (left and right) - P11000-R & L
18	Brush - PA11684
	Brush Holder - P10132
19	Field Assembly - XA13A036
20	Yoke Assembly - XA13A037
21	Field Clamp - PA13A034
22	Set Screw - S165
23	Screw - S4A06
24	Armature - XA14B873-RP
25	Truck Chassis - XA12A074-RP
	Pul Mor Wheel Assembly - XA14A891
	Pul Mor - PA14A890
	Solid Wheel - PA14B888
	Axle - PA15A281
	Worm Gear - PA15A218
	Thrust Plate - PA11463
26	Truck - XA13A809-B
	Truck & Coupler Assembly (parts 26,28,29 and 30) - XA13A810-B
28	Coupler Assembly - XA12A047
29	Leaf Spring - PA12A355-A
30	Tubular Rivet - PA13A791
31	Screw - S249
32	Wheel & Chassis Assembly - XA11598-A
	Not Available - Substitute with XA14A930-A Assembly

NOT SHOWN
Motor Assembly - XA13B038-B
4 Conductor Cable (plastic) - PA13A208-A

10/1/62 NO REVISIONS FOR 371 & 372 UNION PACIFIC

No. 4713 CHIEF LOCOMOTIVE

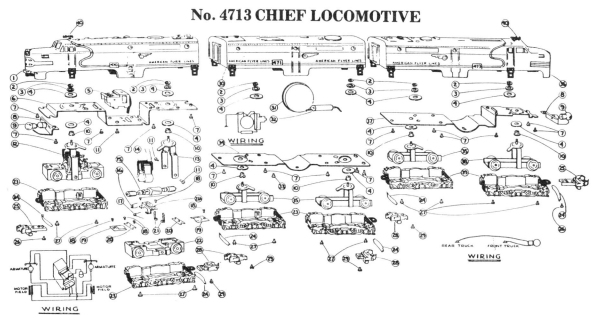

SPECIFICATIONS

Tested at: 12 Volts A.C. ....using 180'' oval of track.
(A) Locomotive to run a minimum of 9 R.P.M. or 9 times forward and reverse, around 180'' oval of track.

Load: Not to draw more than 3.25 amps. while pulling 4 Passenger Cars.

Motor: Universal A.C. or D.C.

6/1/60 PARTS LIST FOR #4713 SANTA FE, #484-485-486 SANTA FE, #490-491-493 NORTHERN PACIFIC, #21902-21902-1-21902-2 SANTA FE AND, #21910-21910-1-21910-2 SANTA FE DIESELS

No.	Description - Part Number
1	Cabin with Trimmings (470) - XA12D075-ARP
	Cabin with Trimmings (484) - XA14B125-RP
	Cabin with Trimmings (490) - XA14B122-RP
	Cabin with Trimmings (21902) - XA15B140-RP
	Cabin with Trimmings (21910) - XA14B125-RP
2	Retaining Ring - P10800-A
3	Washer - W83
	Spring Washer (not used on Old Style 4713) - W2A28
4	Washer - W124
	Steel Washer (not used on Old Style 4713) - W124A
5	Remote Control Unit (used on 470-484-490) - XA10587-E
	Bottom Finger Unit - XA9612-BRP
	Top Finger Unit - XA9612-CRP
	Drum - XA8716
	Remote Control Unit (used on 21902 & 21910)XA14C429
	Contact Assembly - XA14A994
	Plunger Assembly - XA14A435
	Coil Assembly - XA14B433
	Coil Support - PA14A444
	Coil Housing - PA14C432
6	Chassis (used on 470, 484 & 490) - PA11452-B
	Chassis (used on 21902 & 21910) - PA11452-C
7	Screw - S319
8	Lamp Bracket - XA11477
	(used on 470, 473, 484, 486, 490 and 493)
	Lamp Bracket - XA15A383
	(used on 21902, 21902-2, 21910 and 21910-2)
9	Bulb - PA8999
10	Fiber Bushing - PA11455
11	Screw (secures Remote Control Unit) - S172
	Screw (secures Yoke & Field Clamp to Chassis) - S4A06
12	Motor Assembly - XA13B038-B
13	Field Clamp Assembly (4713 only) - XA11457
	(not used with above motor)
	Yoke Assembly - XA13A037

	Field Clamp - PA13A034
	Screw - S165
14	Field Assembly - XA13A036
15	Armature Assembly - XA14B873-RP
16	Brush Spring (left) - P11000-L
17	Brush Spring (right) - P11000-R
18	Screw - S171
19	Worm Cover - PA11441
20	Bearing Strap - PA11453
21	Brush (not sold assembled) - PA11684
	Brush Holder - P10132
22	Truck Chassis Assembly - XA12B065-RP - Not Available
	Use XA12A074-RP Truck Chassis Assembly
	Solid Wheel (Old Style) - PA11343
	Solid Wheel (New Style) - PA14A888
	Insulated Wheel (Old Style)XA11473
	Pul Mor Wheel Assembly (Old Style) - XA12A249
	Pul Mor Wheel Assembly (New Style)XA14A891
	Pul Mor - PA14A890
	Axle - PA15A281
	Worm Gear - PA15A218
	Thrust Plate - PA11463
	Truck with Collector & Coupler Arm Assembly - XA13A803
	(parts 23, 24, 25 and 26)
	Truck with Collector & Coupler Assembly - XA13A804)
	(parts 23, 24, 28 and 29)
23	Truck and Collector Assembly - XA13A802
24	Leaf Spring - PA12A355-A
25	Coupler and Arm Assembly - XA12A358
26	Rivet - PA13A790
27	Screw - S249
	Screw (used on 21902 and 21910)
28	Knuckle Coupler - XA12A047
29	Rivet - PA13A791
30	"B" Unit Cabin (471) - XA11688-BRP
	"B" Unit Cabin (485) - XA11688-GRP

"B" Unit Cabin (491) - XA14B121-RP
"B" Unit Cabin (21902-1) - XA13B875-RP
"B" Unit Cabin (21910-1)XA11688-GRP
31 Speaker - XA11B831 - Not Available
Use XA14A127 Speaker (New Style)
Bracket - PA14A216
Screw - S171
32 Capacitor - PA14A914
33 Screw (Holds Speaker Bracket) - S172
34 Chassis - PA11687
Chassis (used on 21902-1 & 21910-1) - PA11687-D
35 Yoke, Wheel & Chassis Assembly - XA14A930-A
36 "A" Unit Dummy Cabin (473) - XA12D075-ERP
"A" Unit Dummy Cabin (486) - XA14B125-ARP
"A" Unit Dummy Cabin (493) - XA14B122-ARP
"A" Unit Dummy Cabin (21902-2) - XA15B140-ARP
"A" Unit Dummy Cabin (21910-2) - XA14B125-ARP
37 Chassis - PA12B059
Chassis (used on 21902-2 & 21910-2)XA13B422
38 Wheel & Chassis Assembly (4713 only) - XA11596-A
Wheel & Chassis Assembly - XA14A930-A
Truck with Coupler Assembly - XA13A801
(parts 24, 28, 29 and 39)

Truck with Coupler Arm Assembly - XA13A800
(parts 24, 25, 26 and 39)
39 Truck Assembly - XA13A799
40 Air Chime (horn) - PA11409

NOT SHOWN
Diesel Sound Generator - PA13A870
Insulating Bushing - PA10209
Washer - P1131-C
8-32 Hex Nut - N25
Lockwasher - P4654
Washer - W55-B
4 Conductor Cable (plastic)(470-484-490)PA13A208A
Lead Wire (21902-21910) - LW-1B1

NO REVISIONS FOR 6/1/60 PARTS LIST FOR #4713 SANTA FE,
#484-485-486 SANTA FE, #490-491,493 NORTHERN PACIFIC,
#21902-21902-1-21902-2 SANTA FE AND, #21910-21910-1-21910-2
SANTA FE DIESELS

BALDWIN DIESEL LOCOMOTIVES:
No. 355, 21801, 21808, 21812, 21813, 21918, 21801-I and 21918-I

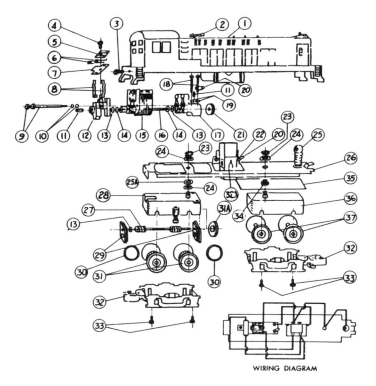

WIRING DIAGRAM

6/1/60 PARTS LIST FOR #355 BALDWIN DIESEL SWITCHER

No.	Description - Part Number
1	Cab Assembly - XA14B156-RP
	Headlight Lens (Not Shown) - PA14A168
2	Air Chime - PA11409
3	#4 x 1/4" Type "Z" P.K. B.H. Screw - S230B
4	4 -40 x 1/4" Screw - S1
5	Spring Holder - P10118

6 Brush Spring (Right) - PA14A407R
Brush Spring (Left) - PA14A407L
7 Brush Mount - PA14A169
8 Brush Holder (Not Sold Assembled) - PA14A588
Brush - PA14A414
9 4 - 40 Shoulder Screw - S4A82
10 Lock Washer - W57
11 Oil Wick - PA9522
12 Brush & Bearing Cap - XA14B162-ARP
13 Washer - PA1405 D
14 Fiber Washer - P325D
15 Field Assembly - XA14A969-A
16 Armature Assembly - XA14B862
17 Bearing & Mount Assembly - XA15A777
18 4 - 40 Phillips Hd. Screw - S4A81A
19 Lock Washer - W46
20 Terminal - PA6173
21 24 Tooth Gear - PA14A586
22 #4 X 3/16" Type "Z" B.H. P.K. Screw - S172
23 Retaining Ring - P10800B
24 Spring Washer - W114
25 14 Volt Bulb - PA8999
25A Steel Washer - W7
26 Chassis & Lamp Socket Assembly - XA14A730
27 Worm Shaft & Gear Assembly - XA14A638
28 Chassis & Stud Assembly (powered only) - XA14A729
Collector Button - PA14A171
Collector Spring - PA14A597
Retaining Ring - P10434
29 Worm Shaft Bearing - PA14A165
30 Pul Mor Tire - PA14A890
31 Pul Mor Wheel Axle & Gear - XA14A933
Pul Mor Wheel Asembly (insulated) - XA14A891
Axle - PA15A255
20 Tooth Gear - PA15A218
32 Truckside & Coupler Assembly - XA14A148
Leaf Spring - PA12A355-A
Rivet - PA13A791
Knuckle Coupler - XA12A047

NO.	Description - Part Numbers		
32A	Remote Control Assembly - XA10587-E	36	Chassis & Stud Assembly (not powered) - XA15A706
	Bottom Finger Unit - XA9612BRP	37	Wheel & Axle Assembly (front truck) - XA14A932
	Top Finger Unit - XA9612CRP		Solid Wheel - PA14B888
	Drum - XA8716		Truck Axle - PA15A226
33	#2 x 3/16" Type "Z" B.H. P.K. Screw - S171		Insulated Wheel Assembly - XA14A870
34	Insulating Bushing - PA10209		
35	Insulating Strip - PA14A100		

10/1/62 NO REVISIONS FOR #355 BALDWIN DIESEL SWITCHER

6/1/60 PARTS LIST FOR #21801 NORTHWESTERN W/R. C., #21812 T. & P. and #21918 SEABOARD DIESELS

NO.	Description - Part Numbers		
1	Cab Assembly (#21801) - XA14B156RP	27	Worm Shaft & Gear Assembly - XA14A638
	Cab Assembly (#21918) - XA14B156ARP	28	Chassis & Stud Assembly (Powered Only) - XA14A729
	Cab Assembly (#21812) - XA14B156-CRP		Collector Button - PA14A171
	Headlight Lens (not shown) - PA14A168		Collector Spring - PA14A597
2	Air Chime - PA11409		Retaining Ring - P10434
3	#4 x 1/4" Type "Z" P.K.B.H. Screw - S230B	29	Worm Shaft Bearing - PA14A165
4	4 - 40 x 1/4" Screw - S1	30	Pul Mor Tire - PA14A890
5	Spring Holder - P10118	31	Pul Mor Wheel Axle & Gear - XA14A933
6	Brush Spring (Right) - PA14A407R		Pul Mor Wheel Assembly (insulated) - XA14A891
	Brush Spring (Left) - PA14A407L		Axle - PA15A225
7	Brush Mount - PA14A169		20 Tooth Gear - PA15A218
8	Brush Holder (Not Sold Assembled) - PA14A588	32	Truckside & Coupler Assembly - XA14A148
	Brush - PA14A414		Leaf Spring - PA12A355-A
9	4 - 40 Shoulder Screw - S4A82		Rivet - PA13A791
10	Lock Washer - W57		Knuckle Coupler - XA12A047
11	Oil Wick - PA9522	32A	2 Position Remote Control - XA14C429
12	Brush & Bearing Cap - XA14B162ARP		Coil Housing - PA14C432
13	Washer - PA1405D		Coil Support - PA14A444
14	Fiber Washer - P325D		Coil Assembly - XA14B433
15	Field Assembly - XA14A969-A		Plunger - XA14A435
16	Armature Assembly - XA14B862		Contact - XA14A994
17	Bearing & Mount Assembly - XA15A777	33	#2 x 3/16" Type "Z" B.H.P.K. Screw - S171
18	4 - 40 Phillips Hd. Screw - S4A81A	34	Insulating Bushing - PA10209
19	Lock Washer - W46	35	Insulating Strip - PA14A100
20	Terminal - PA6173	36	Chassis & Stud Assembly (Not Powered) - XA15A706
21	24 Tooth Gear - PA14A586	37	Wheel & Axle Assembly (Front Truck) - XA14A932
22	#4 x 3/16" Type "Z", B.H.P.K. Screw - S172		Solid Wheel - PA14B888
23	Retaining Ring - P10800B		Truck Axle - PA15A226
24	Spring Washer - W114		Insulated Wheel Assembly - XA14A870
25	14 Volt Bulb - PA8999		
25A	Steel Washer - W7		
26	Chassis & Lamp Socket Assembly - XA15A147		

10/1/61 NO REVISIONS FOR #21801 NORTHWESTERN W/R.C.
#21812 T. & P. AND #21918 SEABOARD DIESELS

6/1/60 PARTS LIST FOR #21808 NORTHWESTERN DIESEL AND #21813 MISSOURI & ST. LOUIS DIESEL

No.	Description - Part Number		
1	Cab Assembly (21808) - XA15B331-RP	18	4 - 40 Phillips Hd. Screw - S4A81A
	Cab Assembly (21813) - XA15B653-RP	19	Lock Washer - W46
	Headlight Lens (not shown) - PA14A168	20	Terminal - PA6173
2	Air Chime - PA11409		Used on #XA15A777, not used with Remote Control Unit
3	#4 x 1/4" Type "Z" P.K. B.H. Screw - S230B	21	24 Tooth Gear - PA14A586
4	4 - 40 x 1/4" Screw - S1	22	Not Used
5	Spring Holder - P10118	23	Retaining Ring - P10800B
6	Brush Spring (Right) - PA14A407R	24	Spring Washer - W114
	Brush Spring (Left) - PA14A407L	25	Not Used
7	Brush Mount - PA14A169	25A	Steel Washer - W7
8	Brush Holder - PA14A588	26	Chassis - PA14B159B
	Brush (Not Sold Assembled) - PA14A414	27	Worm Shaft & Gear Assembly - XA14A638
9	4 - 40 Shoulder Screw - S4A82	28	Chassis & Stud Assembly (powered only)XA14A729
10	Lock Washer - W57		Collector Button - PA14A171
11	Oil Wick - PA9522		Collector Spring - PA14A597
12	Brush & Bearing Cap - XA14B162ARP		Retaining Ring - P10434
13	Washer - PA1405D	29	Worm Shaft Bearing - PA14A165
14	Fiber Washer - P325D	30	Pul Mor Tire - PA14A890
15	Field Assembly - XA14A969-A	31	Pul Mor Wheel Axle & Gear - XA14A933
16	Armature Assembly - XA14B862		Pul Mor Wheel Assembly (insulated) - XA14A891
17	Bearing & Mount Assembly - XA15A777		Axle - PA15A225
			20 Tooth Gear - PA15A218

32	Truckside & Coupler Assembly - XA14A148
	Leaf Spring - PA12A355-A
	Rivet - PA13A791
	Knuckle Coupler - XA12A047
32A	Switch - PA15A200
	Switch Slide (not shown) - PA15A330
	Switch Rivet (not shown) - P14N305
33	#2 x 3/16" Type "Z" B.H.P.K. Screw - S171
34	Insulating Bushing - PA10209

35	Insulating Strip - PA14A100
36	Chassis & Stud Assembly (Not Powered) - XA15A706
37	Wheel & Axle Assembly (Front Truck) - XA14A932
	Solid Wheel - PA14B888
	Truck Axle - PA15A226
	Insulated Wheel Assembly - XA14A870

10/1/62 NO REVISIONS FOR #21808 NORTHWESTERN AND #21813 MISSOURI & ST. LOUIS DIESELS

6/1/60 PARTS LIST FOR BALDWIN SWITCHER DIESEL [NON- MOTORIZED] AND #21801-1 NORTHWESTERN & #21918-1 SEABOARD

No.	Description - Part Number
1	Cab Assembly (21801-1) - XA14B156-DRP
	Cab Assembly (21918-1) - XA14B156-BRP
	Headlight Lens (Not Shown) - PA14A168
2	Air Chime - PA11409
3	#4 x 1/4" Type "Z" P.K.B.H. Screw - S230-B
Diagram Numbers 4-22 not used on above.	
23	Retaining Ring - P10800B
24	Spring Washer - W114
25	14 Volt Bulb (Used on 21918-1 only)PA8999
25A	Steel Washer - W7
26	Locomotive Chassis (used on 21801-1) - PA14B159C
	Locomotive Chassis (used on 21918-1) - XA15A147
27-31	Not Used

32	Truckside & Coupler Assembly
32A	Not Used
33	Screw - S171
34	Insulating Bushing - PA10209
35	Insulating Strip - PA14A100
36	Chassis and Stud Assembly (used on 21801-1) - XA15A706
	Chassis and Stud Assembly (used on 21918-1) - XA14A729
37	Wheel and Axle Assembly
	Solid Wheel - PA14B888
	Truck Axle - PA15A226
	Insulated Wheel Assembly - XA14A870

NO REVISIONS FOR #21801-1 AND #21918-1

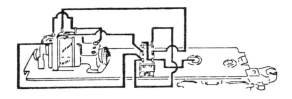

21813 and 21808

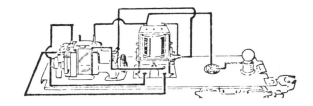

21812 and 21918

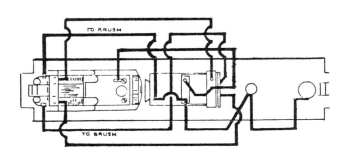

21801 and 355

No. 21088 FRANKLIN AND   No. 21089 WASHINGTON
LOCOMOTIVES AND TENDERS

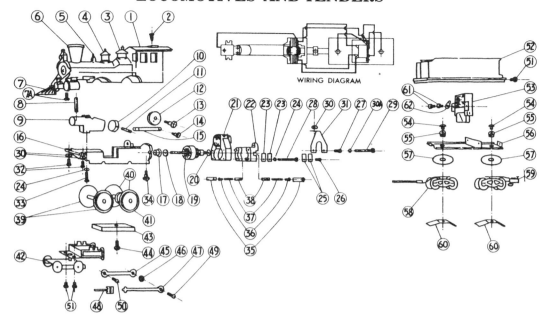

WIRING DIAGRAM

6/1/60 PARTS LIST FOR #21088 OLD TIMER

No.	Description - Part Number
1	Boiler Assembly - XA15B659
2	6 x 3/8" Type "A" Phillips O.H. Screw - S5N48
3	Dome Assembly - XA15A664
4	Sand Box Assembly - XA15A663
5	Bell - PA15A577
6	Smoke Stack - PA15B578
7	Cow Catcher - PA15C582
7A	6 x 7/16" Type "Z" BH. Screw - S306
8	Smoke Tube - P10174-B
9	Smoke Unit Assembly - X13B445-C
10	Carbon Piston - P10053
11	Piston Pin - P10057
12	Worm Gear - PA10A671-A
13	Stud - PA15A021
14	Lever Stud - P10045
15	Piston Rod - PA15A584
16	Chasis - PA15D285-A
17	Rear Bearing - PA13A187
18	Armature Spacer - PA10766
19	Armature Assembly - XA14B719
20	Washer - W-1A92
21	Field Assembly - XA9547-D
22	Brush Mounting Plate Assembly - XA15A695
23	Brush Tube Cover - PA13A129
24	Split Washer - W-57
25	Brush Tube Cover Brace - PA15A044
26	4 x 1/4" Type "F" Rd. Hd. Screw - S240
27	4 x 5/16" Type "F" Rd. Hd. Screw - S264
28	6 x 32 x 1 1/4" Rd. Hd. Screw - S-33
29	6-32 x 1 3/8" Rd. Hd. Screw - S-29
30	Adjusting Roll - P12A062-C
30A	Lockwasher - W-46
31	Bracket - PA15A581
32	6 x 5/16" Type "Z" Rd. Hd. Screw - S-319
33	4 - 40 x 11/16' Rd. Hd. Screw - S-13
34	Shouldered Screw - S5A12
35	Brush Tube - PA13A131
36	Eyelet - P6881
37	Brush Spring - PA13A130

No.	Description - Part Number
38	Motor Brush - PA13A128
39	Flanged Wheel & Axle Assembly - XA15A251-A
	Axle - PA15A226
	Flanged Wheel Assembly - XA14A602-A
40	Pul Mor Wheel Gear & Axle Assembly - XA15A661
	Gear - PA10672
	Axle - PA15A225
	Pul Mor Wheel Assembly - XA15A660
41	Pul Mor - PA14A869
42	Guide and Front Truck Assembly - XA13A085-A
	Crosshead Guide - PA10887
	Tubular Rivet - PA4367
	Front Truck Assembly - XA13A084-A
	Front Truck - PA10081
	Wheel & Axle Assembly - XA13A083-A
	Truck Axle - PA13A082
	Wheel (plastic) - PA9990-E
43	Chassis (lower half) - PA15A286
44	4 - 40 x 1/2" Type "23" Sems. P.K. Screw - S-5N33
45	Side Rod - PA9452
46	Piston Rod Spacer - PA7237
47	Connecting Rod - PA10889
48	Crosshead - PA11099
49	Eccentric Crank Stud - S-5A37
50	Piston Rod Screw - S-5A38
51	4 x 1/4" Type "Z" B.H. Screw - S-230-B
52	Tender Body Assembly - XA15A871RP
53	2 Position Remote Control - XA14C429
	Coil Housing Assembly - PA14A444
	Contact Assembly - XA14A994
	Plunger Assembly - XA14A435
	Coil Assembly - XA14B433
	Coil Support (for Coil and Housing Assembly) - PA14C432
54	Truck Rivet - PA10235-A
55	Insulating Bushing - PA10209
56	Tender Chassis - PA14B385-A
57	Insulating Washer - PA8715-B
58	Front Truck & Draw Bar Assembly - XA15B665
	Draw Bar - PA15A583
	Shouldered Tubular Rivet - P1663

	Front Truck Assembly - XA14B842
59	Truck Assembly - XA12A050-B
	Coupler Assembly - XA12A047
	Wheel & Axle Assembly - XA10238
	Brass Wheel - PA10140
	Wheel (plastic) - PA9990
	Axle - PA10238
60	Contact Spring - PA10207
61	4 x 3/16" Type "Z" Rd. Hd. P.K. Screw - S172
62	Solder Terminal - PA6173

6/1/60 PARTS LIST FOR #21089 WASHINGTON LOCOMOTIVE AND TENDER

Parts differing from #21088 [only]:

No.	Description - Part Number
1	Boiler Assembly - XA15B874RP
52	Tender Body Assembly - XA15A87RP

10/1/62 NO REVISIONS FOR #21088 AND #21089

DOCKSIDER LOCOMOTIVES
Nos. 21155, 21156 AND 21158

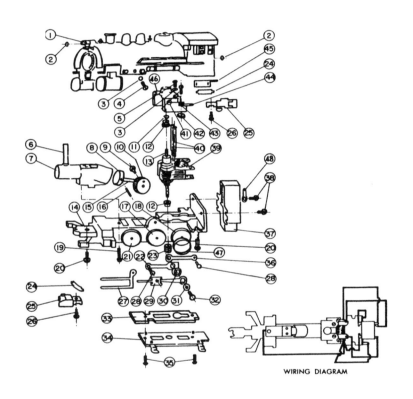

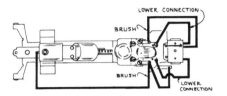

21155 DOCKSIDE

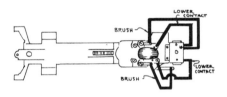

21156 DOCKSIDE

WIRING DIAGRAM

6/1/60 PARTS LIST FOR #21155

No.	Description - Part Number
1	Boiler Assembly - XA15DOOO-RP
2	Lamp Insert - P14A653
3	Fiber Washer - PA131OC
4	4 - 40 x 1/4" R. H. Screw - S1
5	3 - 48 Shoulder Screw - S5A34
6	Smoke Tube - P10174-B
7	Smoke Unit Assembly - X13B445-A
8	Piston - P10053
9	Stud - PA15A021
10	22 Tooth Gear - PA15A019
11	Fiber Washer - W2A40
12	Bearing - PA14A164-B
13	Armature Assembly - XA15B024
14	Chassis, Bearing and Spring Assembly - XA14N999-RP
15	Piston Rod - P10052
16	Piston Pin - P10057
17	Flangeless Wheel & Axle Assembly - XA15A221-A
	Flangless Wheel with stud - PA15B033
	Axle - PA15A226

No.	Description - Part Number
18	Pul Mor Wheel Gear & Axle Assembly - XA15A220
	Pul Mor Wheel Assembly - XA15A035
	Axle - PA15A225
	20 Tooth Gear - PA15A218
19	4 - 40 x 1/2" Type 43 Sems Screw - S5N33
20	4 x 3/8" Type "Z" P.K.B.H. Screw - S181
21	Flanged Wheel & Axle Assembly - XA15A219
	Flanged Wheel - PA15C031
	Axle - PA15A226
22	Side Rod (Front)PA15A016
23	Worm - PA15A224
24	Leaf Spring - PA12A355A
25	Coupler Assembly - XA12A047
26	#4 Self Tapping Shoulder Screw - S5A29
27	Crosshead Guide (Right and Left) - PA10595 R & L
28	Piston Rod Screw - S5A38
29	Crosshead Assembly - XA15A008
30	Piston Rod Spacer - PA7237-A
31	Fiber Washer - PA1310C

32	Eccentric Crank Screw - S5A37
33	Chassis Lower Half - PA15B223
34	Pick Up Assembly - XA15B222
	Contact - PA15A176
	Contact (Formed) - PA15A176A
	Pick Up Shoe - PA15B178
	Pick Up Shoe - PA15B178A
35	#2 x 1/2" Type "Z" P.K. Screw - S4N30
36	Side Rod (Rear) - PA15A015
37	2 Position Remote Control - XA14C429
	Coil Housing Assembly - PA14A444
	Contact Assembly - XA14A994
	Plunger Assembly - XA14A435
	Coil Assembly - XA14B4333
	Coil Support (For Coil & Housing Assembly) - PA14C432
38	#4 x 3/16" Type "Z" P.K.B.H. Screw - S172
39	Field Assembly - XA15A017
40	4 - 40 Shoulder Screw - S5A30
41	Brush - PA14A917
42	#3 - 48 Pal Nut - N75
43	Brush Spring (Right & Left) - PA14A919 R & L
44	Solder Terminal - PA10059
45	Coupler Bracket - PA12A479A
46	Brush Bearing Mount - XA14N916-ARP
47	Pul Mor Tire - PA15A034
48	Solder Terminal - PA6173

6/6/60 PARTS LIST FOR #21156

Parts differing from #21155 only:
No.	Description - Part Number
1	Boiler Assembly - XA15N000-ARP
6-10	Not Used
15-16	Not Used

6/1/60 PARTS LIST FOR #21158

Parts differing from #21155 and #21156 only:
No.	Description - Part Number
1	Boiler Assembly - XA15A000-BRP
2	Not Used
6-10	Not Used
15-16	Not Used
17	Flangeless Wheel & Axle Assembly - XA15A221-B
18	Pul Mor Wheel Gear & Axle Assembly - XA15A220-A
	Pul Mor Wheel - XA15A035-A
21	Flanged Wheel & Axle Assembly - XA15A219-A
	Flanged Wheel - PA15C031-B
25	Knuckle Coupler (solid) - PA15B215
34	Pick Up Assembly - XA16B086

10/1/62 NO REVISIONS FOR #21155, 21156 or 21158

No. 21165 AND No. 21168 LOCOMOTIVES AND TENDERS

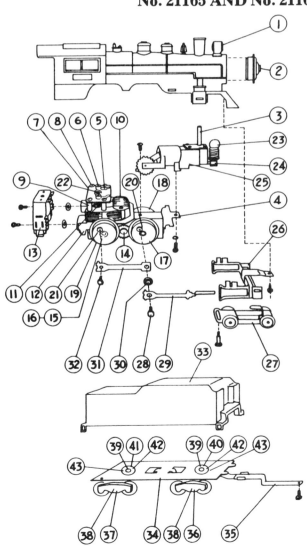

4/23/62 PARTS LIST FOR #21165 LOCOMOTIVE & TENDER

No.	Description - Part Number
1	Boiler Assembly - XA30N165
	Plug - P30A163
2	Boiler Front - PA30C048
3	Not Used
4	Motor & Chassis Assembly - XA30C047
5	Brush Spring - PA16A380
6	Motor Brush - PA30A032
7	Brush Plate Assembly - XA30A033
8	6-32 x 7/8 Rd. Hd. Screw - S-24
9	Spacer - PA30A034
10	Field Assembly - XA30A167
11	Armature Assembly - XA30B168
	Washer - P325A
12	Chassis, Wheel, Axle & Gear Assembly - XA30N062
	Worm Gear Axle - PAl5A225
	Plain Axle - PA15A226
13	Remote Control Unit - XA14C429
	Contact Assembly - XA14A994
	Plunger Assembly - XA14A435
	Coil Assembly - XA14B433
	Coil Support - PA14A444
	Coil Housing - PA14C432
14	Chassis & Idler Gear Assembly - XA30N061
15	Drive Wheel - PA30C042
16	Flanged Wheel with stud - PA14C867-B
17	Pul Mor Wheel Only - XA14A913-A
18	Pul Mor Drive Wheel Only - XA30N064
19	Pul Mor - PA14A869
20	Wheel Bearing - PA30A039
21	Helical Gear - PA30A025
22	Motor Bearing - PA30A021*
23	Not Used
24	Not Used
25	Not Used
26	Side Rod Guide (not illustrated on diagram) - PA30A024
27	Pilot Truck Assembly - XA30A035
28	Piston Rod Screw - S5A38

No.	Description - Part Number
29	Piston Rod (not illustrated on diagram) - PA30A017
30	Not Used
31	Not Used
32	Not Used
33	Tender Body - PA12A078-E
	Screw - S222
34	Tender Chassis - PA30A052
35	Draw Bar Extension - PA30A053
36	Truck & Wheel Assembly - XA30A051
	Wheel & Axle Assembly - XA10238
37	Truck & Wheel Assembly - XA30A050
	Wheel & Axle Assembly - XA10238

No.	Description - Part Number
38	Contact Spring - PA30A164
39	Eyelet - P10A987
40	Washer - W6A
41	Washer - W6B
42	Fiber Sleeve - PA30A020
43	Fiber Washer - W2A43

*When inserting bearing on brush plate (Bubble #7) be sure head of bearing does not short circuit the brush tubes.

10/1/62 NO REVISIONS FOR #21165 LOCOMOTIVE AND TENDER

4/23/62 PARTS LIST FOR #21168 LOCOMOTIVE AND TENDER

No.	Description - Part Number
1	Boiler Assembly - XA30N166
	Plug - P30A163
	Headlight Lens - PA30A117
2	Boiler Front - PA30C048
3	Smoke Stack - P10174-B
4	Motor & Chassis Assembly - XA30C118
5	Brush Spring - PA16A380
6	Motor Brush - PA30A032
7	Brush Plate Assembly - XA30A033
8	6-32 x 1" Rd. Hd. Screw - S-20
9	Spacer - PA30A034
10	Field Assembly - XA9547-E
11	Armature Assembly - XA30B044
	Washer - P325A
12	Chassis, Wheel, Axle & Gear Assembly - XA30N062-A
	Worm Gear Axle - PA15A225
	Plain Axle - PA15A226
13	Remote Control Unit - XA14C429
	Contact Assembly - XA14A994
	Plunger Assembly - XA14A435
	Coil Assembly - XA14B433
	Coil Support - PA14A444
	Coil Housing - PA14C432
14	Chassis & Idler Gear Assembly - XA30N061-A
15	Pul Mor Drive Wheel - XA30N064
	Pul Mor - PA14A869
16	Pul Mor Wheel - XA14A913-A
17	Drive Wheel - PA30C042
18	Flanged Wheel with stud - PA14C867-B
19	Pul Mor - PA14A869

No.	Description - Part Number
20	Wheel Bearing - PA30A039
21	Helical Gear - PA30A025
22	Motor Bearing - PA30A021*
23	Lamp - PA8999
24	Headlight Clip Assembly - XA16A500
25	Smoke Unit Assembly - XA30B105
26	Crosshead Guide & Bracket - XA16A537
27	Pilot Truck Assembly - XA30A035
28	Piston Rod Screw - S5A38
29	Main Rod - PA30A116
30	Piston Rod Spacer - PA7237
31	Side Rod - PA30C115
32	Eccentric Crank Screw - S5A37
33	Tender Body - PA12A078-F
	Screw - S222
34	Tender Chasis - PA30A052
35	Draw Bar Extension - PA30A053
36	Truck & Wheel Assembly - XA30A051
	Wheel & Axle Assembly - XA10238
37	Truck & Wheel Assembly - XA30A050
	Wheel & Axle Assembly - XA10238
38	Contact Spring - PA30A164
39	Eyelet - P10A987
40	Washer - W6A
41	Washer - W6B
42	Fiber Sleeve- PA30A020
43	Fiber Washer - W2A43

*When inserting bearing on brush plate (Bubble #7) be sure head of bearing does not short circuit the brush tubes.

10/1/62 NO REVISIONS FOR #21168 LOCOMOTIVE AND TENDER

DIESEL LOCOMOTIVES
21205, 21206, 21210, 21215,
21215-I, 21205-I, 21206-I, L2004 AND L2004-I

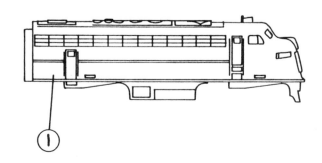

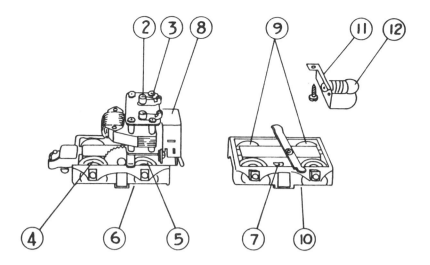

4/16/62 PARTS LIST FOR #21205, #21210, #21215 DIESEL LOCOMOTIVES AND #21215-1 DIESEL DUMMY A [NOT MOTORIZED] LOCOMOTIVE

No.	Description - Part Number
1	Cabin (Boston & Maine) - XA30N071-ARP
	Cabin (Burlington) - XA30N071-HRP
	Cabin (Union Pacific) - XA30N071-BRP
	Cabin (Union Pacific) - XA30N071-CRP
2	Brush - PA30A032
3	Brush Spring - PA16A380
4	Wheel, Axle, Gear and Bearing Assembly - XA30A091
	Pul Mor - PA15A034

No.	Description - Part Number
5	Wheel, Axle and Bearing Assembly - XA30A095
6	Bottom Plate Assembly - XA30A089
7	Collector Assembly - XA30A078
8	Remote Control Assembly - XA140429
9	Wheel and Axle Assembly - XA30A073
10	Bottom Plate Assembly)with coupler) - XA30A076
11	Lamp Bracket Assembly - XA15158-A
12	Bulb - PA8999

10/1/62 REVISIONS FOR #21205, #21206, #21210, #21215 AND #L-2004 DIESEL A LOCOMOTIVES

Changes only listed below:

No.	Description - Part Number
1	Cabin (Boston & Maine) 21205 - XA30N071-ARP
	Cabin (Burlington) 21210 - XA30N071-HRP
	Cabin (Union Pacific) 21215 - XA30N071-BRP
	Cabin (Santa Fe) 21206 - XA30B071-ABRP
	Cabin (Rio Grande) L2004 - XA30B071-ACRP
2	Brush - PA30A032
3	Brush Spring - PA16A380
4	Wheel, Axle, Gear & Bearing Assembly - XA30A091
	Pul Mor - PA15A034
5	Wheel, Axle & Bearing Assembly - XA30A095
6	Bottom Plate Assembly (motor end) - XA30A089
7	Collector Assembly - XA30A078
8	Remote Control Assembly - XA14C429
	Contact Assembly - XA14A994
	Plunger Assembly - XA14A435

	Description - Part Number
	Coil Assembly - XA14B433
	Coil Support - PA14A444
	Coil Housing - PA14C432
9	Wheel and Axle Assembly - XA30A073
10	Bottom Plate Assembly with coupler - XA30A076
	Bottom Plate (no coupler) (L2004 - 21205 - 21206) - PA30B077
11	Lamp Bracket Assembly (used on 21210 and 21215) - XA15158-A
12	Bulb (used on 21210 and 21215) - PA8999
Not Shown	
	Truck Body Assembly with gear (motor end) - XA30102
	Plastic Truck Frame (motor end) - PA30D072-A
	Field Assembly - XA9547-E
	Armature - XA30083
	Brush Plate Assembly - XA30A033
	Truck Body Assembly (front) - XA30103
	Plastic Truck Frame (front) - PA30D072
	6 x 5/16 Type "Z" P.K. Screw for Lamp Bracket - S319

10/1/62 PARTS REVISIONS LIST FOR #L-2004-1, #21205-1, #21206-1 AND #21215-1 DUMMY A UNITS [NOT MOTORIZED]

Changes only listed below:

No.	Description - Part Number
1	Cabin for L2004-1 - XA30N071-CDRP
	Cabin for 21205-1 - XA30B071-CCRP
	Cabin for 21206-1 - XA30B071-CBRP
	Cabin for 21215-1 - XA30B071-CARP
2, 3	Not Used
4, 5	Wheel and Axle Assembly - XA30A073

No.	Description - Part Number
6	Metal Bottom Plate Assembly)with coupler) - XA30A076
	Knuckle Coupler - XA12A047
7, 8	Not Used
9	Wheel and Axle Assembly - XA30A073
10	Metal Bottom Plate Assembly with knuckle coupler - XA30A076
	Knuckle Coupler - XA12A047
11, 12	Not Used

Roundhouse Records

Engine	Date	Repairs/Maintenance